The Manager's Tool Kit

The Manager's Tool Kit

Practical Tips for Tackling 100 On-the-Job Problems

Cy Charney

amacom

American Management Association

New York • Atlanta • Boston • Chicago • Kansas City • San Francisco • Washington, D.C.
Brussels • Mexico City • Tokyo • Toronto

This book is available at a special
discount when ordered in bulk quantities.
For information, contact Special Sales Department,
AMACOM, a division of American Management Association,
1601 Broadway, New York, NY 10019.

This publication is designed to provide accurate and authoritative information in regard to the subject matter covered. It is sold with the understanding that the publisher is not engaged in rendering legal, accounting, or other professional service. If legal advice or other expert assistance is required, the services of a competent professional person should be sought.

Library of Congress Cataloging-in-Publication Data

Charney, Cyril.
    The manager's tool kit : practical tips for tackling 100 on-the
-job problems / Cy Charney. — 1st U.S. ed.
      p.   cm.
    Includes index.
    ISBN 0-8144-7881-6
    1. Management—Handbooks, manuals, etc.   2. Problem solving-
-Handbooks, manuals, etc.   I. Title.
HD38.15.C48   1995
658.4'03—dc20   94-41742
                                                           CIP

First U.S. edition, 1995.
A previous edition of this book was published in Canada by
Stoddart Publishing Co., Ltd., Ontario,
under the title The Instant Manager.

Printing number

10

Is there a person alive richer than me? At home, I am blessed with love, support, and caring. At work, I am surrounded by people of integrity, who stimulate and challenge me. So, I dedicate this book to all the people in my life.

Contents

Preface

This book is designed to enable you to access quickly the tools you need to be an effective manager. Perhaps you have attended many training sessions but need to brush up on selected skills. Or you need a mentor, guide, and reminder that will give you rapid information to improve your daily performance.

In developing this book I have relied on the tools that my clients, associates, and I have taught managers in Canada, the United States, Europe, and Africa. My approach has been pragmatic—short on theory and long on workable ideas.

Throughout I have assumed that you operate from a similar philosophy about people as I do: namely, that most people are responsible, do want to contribute to the goals of the organization, are loyal, and want to expand their knowledge and influence. Sadly, although organizations I come across typically say they believe people do feel this way, in practice, their management styles often reflect distrust. No wonder organizational performance is so poor. Employees' lack of enthusiasm and initiative can usually be traced to the leaders of the organization. To overcome this contradictory characteristic of organizations, people in positions of authority need to spend more time empowering people and less time talking about it. I hope this book will help.

Acknowledgments

To ensure that my ideas are relevant to the needs of managers today, I have sought the counsel of a number of human resources professionals and line managers. I am indebted to these professionals for their ideas and advice.

Absenteeism

Absenteeism costs everyone. It increases your costs by necessitating the hiring of temporary staff and paying for increased overtime. It reduces your customer service since fill-in staff are less effective. And it aggravates fellow employees who are often called upon to pick up the slack. You cannot avoid some absenteeism. But levels of above 10 percent indicate a serious problem; levels below 5 percent are good. If you have a problem, here's how you can turn it around:

- Keep statistics to pinpoint problems and trends. Your data log should tell you:
  - ✓ Who was absent
  - ✓ When they were absent
  - ✓ Why they were absent
- Compare your area to other similar work areas. Find out if your people are:
  - ✓ Better than average
  - ✓ Average
  - ✓ Worse than average
- Analyze your data. Look for applications of the 80/20 principle. You may find that:
  - ✓ 20 percent of your people are absent 80 percent of the time
  - ✓ 80 percent of the absenteeism occurs on 20 percent of the days
  - ✓ 20 percent of the causes account for 80 percent of the time off
- Let your people know that you are aware of and concerned about the problem.
- Ask them to help you identify the most critical causes. See if you can make improvements. Things you can improve include:
  - ✓ Boredom
  - ✓ Monotony
  - ✓ Lack of reward
  - ✓ Lack of challenge

✓ Lack of responsibility
✓ Lack of feedback
Items you have little or no control over include:
✓ Personal problems
✓ Sickness
✓ Family problems (sick child, bereavement)
- Deal with absenteeism immediately, whether your associate has been away for one day or one month. Interview the persons when they get back to find out why. Show your interest and concern.
- Let new associates know your attitude towards absenteeism during orientation as well as the company's policies and procedures. While your approach should not be threatening, people should know that the consequences may be:
✓ Loss of pay
✓ Hostility of peers who have to fill in or do extra work
✓ A note in their personnel record
✓ Demotion
✓ Termination
- Be consistent and follow company guidelines, but show empathy for those who are having a legitimate temporary problem. Work with them to get them back on track.
- Focus your energy on those associates who are responsible for the most absenteeism. Typically, 20 percent of your people account for 80 percent of the problem.

Accidents

Employers have both moral and legal obligations to safe-guard the health, safety, and welfare of all employees at work insofar as it is reasonable and practical. Employees should take reasonable care of themselves and others, and cooperate with their employer on matters of health and safety. While your task is first to prevent accidents, here is what you should do if they occur:

- Check if there is risk of further injuries. If so, clear the area. Instruct people to vacate the building if necessary.
- Assess the nature of the accident. Evaluate whether you are capable of dealing with the injury.
- If the injury is serious, call for emergency assistance. While you are waiting for help:
  ✓ Keep the injured person warm and quiet
  ✓ Be reassuring
  ✓ Do not show that you are afraid or overly concerned
  ✓ Keep the area around injured people as quiet as possible
- If the injury is minor, send the employee for appropriate first aid. Someone in your organization must be trained in these procedures and must be available at all times.
- Make a record of the accident. Even minor accidents can develop into serious conditions. Inadequate documentation can cause difficulty in establishing a claim.
- Report the accident to your company's human resources department or risk manager, who will process any claim for workers compensation, including loss of time away from the job for medical treatment.

Anger

Anger is a natural part of life. Like conflict, anger can be positive if it mobilizes energy to overcome obstacles. But if it is focused on people it can be destructive. These ideas will help you reduce the negative effects of anger.

Your Own

- Acknowledge your anger.
- Identify the source of your anger. Is this person or event the real source of your anger or just a trigger for unresolved, and perhaps unrelated, anger?
- Act, don't react. Focus on events, actions, and things, not on the person.
- If you feel out of control, take a deep breath, count to ten, and try to respond as calmly as possible. If this is difficult, leave the situation until you feel ready to deal with it calmly and rationally. Talk to a third person first if necessary.
- If you are documenting your concerns, and others will read your notes, don't send the first draft. Wait 24 hours to review your tone and choice of language. If possible, have a trusted and objective colleague edit your work.

From Others

- Listen when others vent their anger.
- Allow them to finish so that they have everything off their chests.
- Acknowledge their right to be angry.
- Confirm your agreement and understanding with issues verbally or by nodding.
- Don't use language that might trigger further anger.
- Maintain a calm, quiet posture and speak in a calm tone (measured volume and pace).

- Help the person deal with the problem so that it does not recur.
- Ask the person to document more complex problems. Set up a time to review concerns.

Assertiveness

To know how to refuse is as important as to know how to consent.

Baltassar Gracian

Being assertive does not mean being aggressive. And it does not mean always saying what's on your mind regardless of whom you hurt, or always getting your own way. Assertiveness is truthful, open, nonjudgmental communication that expresses one's own needs. Assertive people feel good about themselves, act appropriately, and take responsibility.

- Learn the difference between assertiveness and aggression. Aggression focuses on the person who is frustrating your needs. Assertiveness on the other hand focuses on the problem.
- Learn to say no without feeling guilty.
- Even though being assertive can be emotionally difficult (your heart may be racing and your palms sweaty), don't lose control.
- Maintain a well-balanced, erect, and relaxed posture. Keep your eyes open and direct without staring.
- Speak in a firm voice that suggests you are sure of yourself.
- Describe the situation, what's happening now. For example, "This letter has three typing errors."
- Express your true feelings, your likes and dislikes, using *I* statements. For example, "I am really upset that the letter was sent out with three mistakes." It makes your wishes and expectations clear without putting the other person on the defensive.
- Get your point across without getting involved in side issues.
- Use the broken record technique: Repeat the message, to avoid being manipulated and sidetracked.

- Be specific about what you want and describe the consequences if the goal is not achieved.
- Do not begin a refusal with an apology. Say no firmly and keep your explanation short and clear.
- Express your case with conviction, but do not neglect the position of the other person. Be prepared to listen and be influenced. Concede any reasonable points, but disagree with issues you find unacceptable.

ASSERTIVENESS CHECKLIST

Do you need to improve your assertiveness? Check the box that best describes how you feel about the following issues:

	Yes	No
• I get apologetic if I don't have an answer for my boss right away.	❏	❏
• I need to apologize to those who don't agree with my decisions.	❏	❏
• I don't have the right to change my mind.	❏	❏
• I have to help everyone who needs me.	❏	❏
• I feel guilty when I make mistakes even if I can fix them.	❏	❏
• I don't have the right to ask someone to change their behavior towards me.	❏	❏
• I feel foolish when I don't understand my boss.	❏	❏
• I don't have the right to postpone activities that appear less important.	❏	❏
• I don't have the right to say no to things I cannot or do not want to do.	❏	❏
• I don't have the right to walk away from an argument.	❏	❏
• I don't have the right to be heard, especially if my view is very different from the majority.	❏	❏
• I don't have the right to question instructions.	❏	❏

Key: If you answer YES to:

8-11	You need significant improvement.
4-7	You need improvement.
0-3	You are taking care of yourself.

Attitude Survey

Research shows a direct correlation between people's attitudes and their effectiveness on the job. So if you improve your people's morale, you are likely to improve customer satisfaction. Although morale can be measured by staff turnover and absenteeism, neither of these indicators will pinpoint the cause of the problem. An excellent method of collecting accurate data and establishing specific causes is through a survey. Here is what you need to do.

Before the Survey

- Research survey methods and sources thoroughly before deciding whether to get outside help or to construct and conduct a survey in-house. Your decision will be based on:
  ✓ Cost
  ✓ Reliability (produces similar results again and again)
  ✓ Validity (tracks what it purports to measure)
  ✓ Comprehensiveness (measures a variety of subjects)
- Using an outside resource will have pros and cons. The cons might include costs, but the benefits will include:
  ✓ Professional advice
  ✓ Proven surveys
  ✓ Industry benchmark data
  ✓ Sophisticated software permitting manipulation of data for analysis
  ✓ An easily understood feedback package
  ✓ Time savings
  ✓ Generic or customized surveys
  ✓ Confidentiality

Preparing a Survey

- Determine which subjects to measure. For example:
  ✓ Recognition
  ✓ Communications

✓ Relationship with boss
✓ Confidence in management
✓ Career development
✓ Job satisfaction
✓ Training and career opportunities
✓ Compensation and benefits
- Decide whether to collect information with open- or closed-ended questions. The latter are typically scored with a Likert scale, which has five possible responses:
  ✓ Strongly disagree
  ✓ Disagree
  ✓ Neither agree nor disagree
  ✓ Agree
  ✓ Strongly agree
- Set a date for conducting the survey. In order to get the highest level of participation, conduct the survey in-house, during work hours. Surveys rarely take more than 45 minutes.
- Let people know about the survey three to seven days in advance. Your method of communication should depend on the number of people and the level of trust. The more suspicious your people are of your intentions, the greater the advantage of using direct communication. Either way, people should be told about:
  ✓ The purpose
  ✓ The process to implement, disseminate, and use the data
  ✓ The date, time, and place of the survey
  ✓ How confidentiality will be protected
  ✓ How people will be able to access the data
- Tell people you intend to share results and to use the information to make changes. People will be more inclined to participate.

During the Survey

- Use a quiet, appropriately sized meeting room or schedule people throughout the day if the sample is large.
- Before the survey begins, explain why you are conducting it and how to complete it. Allow time for questions. Emphasize

that the process is voluntary. If people are not convinced about the benefit or confidentiality, allow them to exclude themselves by leaving or spoiling their questionnaire.
- Seat people a reasonable distance apart so that they cannot see others' responses.
- Give people ample time to complete the survey. Allow them to leave when finished. Thank them for participating.

After the Survey

- Analyze the data. Develop graphs to show highlights, trends, and comparisons.
- Review the results with management. Plan to share the information with staff. Decide:
  ✓ How to communicate the information
  ✓ When it will be done
  ✓ What information to provide
- Communicate results of the survey to all employees in a format that they can easily understand. A personal presentation with charts and graphs should be supplemented with a written summary.
- Develop plans for improvement with employees' input.
- Continue to improve morale by solving new problems as they arise, so that people will see that you are sincere about dealing with their concerns. Evaluate your success when you next do a survey, one year after the first.
- Conduct focus groups with staff where clarification is needed or where there is value in defining the problems specific to a particular department. Consider using a nonpartisan facilitator to get the most useful information.

Benchmarking

Benchmarking is the continuous process of measuring products, services, and practices against the toughest competitors or those companies regarded as leaders.

David T. Kearns, CEO, Xerox Corporation

Benchmarking enables your organization or your work area to identify how good you could be. It then requires that you take action to become at least as good as the best. This is how you can do it.

Develop a Plan

- Identify what you want to benchmark. The answer might be obvious if you have:
  - ✓ Increased customer complaints
  - ✓ Reduced sales
  - ✓ Falling market share
  - ✓ Returns
  - ✓ Sharply increased costs
- Identify what information you need from your survey of issues and concerns. Your information may be related to:
  - ✓ Quality (doing it right the first time)
  - ✓ Responsiveness (doing it quickly)
  - ✓ Cost effectiveness (cost ratios, profit margins)
  - ✓ Health and safety
  - ✓ Staff morale
- Determine who should collect the information. At least two people should be involved to ensure objectivity and accuracy. The team should include people who:
  - ✓ Will have to implement the changes

    ✓ Have experience in benchmarking and data collection
    ✓ Have the power to authorize change
- Decide how the data will be collected. You may do this by:
    ✓ Telephone interviews
    ✓ A written survey
    ✓ Direct observation
- Decide how to record the data. You might need to design appropriate:
    ✓ Checksheets to collect data
    ✓ Questions you need to ask
    ✓ Surveys
- Identify sources of the data. Sources could be from:
    ✓ Within your own organization (always the easiest, but often overlooked)
    ✓ A competitor
    ✓ Conferences
    ✓ Literature (published papers, articles, books)
    ✓ Staff who have worked at competitors
    ✓ Industry associations

Organize

- Hold a team meeting to review your preliminary plan. Listen to their ideas and fine-tune the plan if necessary.
- Make contact with sources of information. Offer them the possibility of data sharing as an incentive to providing you with information.

Implement

- Conduct your data collection as planned.

Analyze

- Tabulate your data to identify:
    ✓ The area(s) of poor performance
    ✓ The extent to which you need to improve

- Analyze why your performance is poor. Causes typically fall into the categories of manpower/staff, methods, machinery/ equipment, and materials.
  The more thorough your research the easier it will be to identify the real, fact-based reason for your performance deficiency.

Plan for Change

- Develop plans to improve the situation. Identify all the actions to be taken, who will do them, and when.
- Set goals that need to be achieved when the action plan is implemented.

Sell Your Plan

- Present your findings, including solutions, goals, and benefits, to anyone who needs to:
  ✓ Implement new procedures
  ✓ Authorize changes in procedures
  ✓ Authorize spending
  The sales presentation is best done by the team who were part of the project from the beginning.

Implement

- Implement your plans. Monitor to make sure that all commitments are being met.

Evaluate Changes

- Measure the benefits. Evaluate whether you have achieved your goal.
- Recognize those people who helped the project and contributed to any improvement.

- Continue finding new ways to improve so that you become the industry leader. Monitor the key indicators of others to make sure that you are competitive. Never become complacent.

Career Change

You have to take control over your own life, or some-one else will do it for you.

It is said that a change is as good as a holiday. But changing careers is anything but a holiday. In fact, it can be very stressful. Here are some ideas to make the transition a little easier:

- Create a list of things you enjoy about your career. If it is a struggle to find anything you really like, you may need a change.
- Develop a list of your career expectations. If you could have any job you wanted:
  - ✓ What would it provide you with?
  - ✓ What kind of tasks would you want to do?
  - ✓ What size organization would you want to work for?
  - ✓ What type of people would you enjoy working with?
  - ✓ How dynamic an environment would best suit you?
- Compare your two lists. Are there important items you are looking for in a job that you do not currently have?
- Create a new list of key needs unmet by your present job.
- Research organizations or departments within your own company that could provide you with more job satisfaction.
- Armed with this information, write down the:
  - ✓ Primary target organization or industry
  - ✓ Second choice target organization or industry
  - ✓ Obstacles to moving to this organization or industry
  - ✓ Steps that must be taken to overcome these obstacles, with dates for achievement
- Imagine yourself in your ideal job. Evaluate it, making a list of pros and cons. Weight each item. Add the scores and draw conclusions about whether you are better off staying or moving.

- Don't be afraid to make a change. The unknown is more frightening than the change itself. Ask yourself, "What is the worst thing that could happen to me?" It probably won't be worse than your current situation. Then ask yourself, "What is the best possible outcome of the change?" The answer will probably give you the adrenaline needed to take the next step.
- Record what an organization needs to offer you in terms of:
  - ✓ Wages
  - ✓ Benefits
  - ✓ Shifts
  - ✓ Location
  - ✓ Transportation
- Discuss the change with your life partner. Evaluate your partner's probable level of support, particularly with the possibility of being jobless for a while.

THINGS TO AVOID IN A JOB INTERVIEW

Your chances of a job offer will be significantly reduced if you:

- ✓ Are not dressed and groomed properly
- ✓ Show little interest in or enthusiasm for the job
- ✓ Criticize your previous employer
- ✓ Emphasize the importance of money
- ✓ Fail to maintain eye contact
- ✓ Project yourself as indecisive, nervous, and ill at ease
- ✓ Fail to project an interest in a career
- ✓ Cannot express yourself clearly
- ✓ Don't speak with a firm, clear voice
- ✓ Project conceit, over-aggressiveness, or superiority
- ✓ Fail to ask about the job
- ✓ Are late for the interview
- ✓ Expect too high a position or salary relative to your background and skills
- ✓ Indicate you are shopping around
- ✓ Fail to complete the application form properly
- ✓ Don't live up to expectations suggested by your resumé
- ✓ Don't provide direct answers to questions

Career Management

My grandfather once told me that there are two kinds of people: those who do the work and those who take the credit. He told me to try to be in the first group; there was less competition there.

INDIRA GANDHI

No one can manage your career better than you can. But if you sit around waiting for opportunities to present themselves you may sit around forever. You must be proactive. You must be assertive. The following ideas will improve your chances of moving up the corporate ladder:

- Be a team player and make your best effort to shine on the team. Encourage others to reach team goals on time and within budget.
- Volunteer for high-profile projects. Doing so will increase your exposure to key decision makers.
- Stay out of political camps. If you have to make a choice, wait as long as you can to increase your chances of backing the winner.
- Conduct yourself with integrity. Tell the truth no matter how difficult it may be.
- Always work collaboratively. Running others down or refusing to cooperate will only lead to senseless conflict. Your chances of a promotion are slim when you are continuously in the center of controversy.
- Think like a top manager. Stay in tune with the "hot buttons" of the day and find ways to help meet corporate objectives. If there are critical roadblocks preventing the organization from moving forward, look for ways in which these can be removed.
- Establish a joint vision with your boss of your career objectives and the road by which you will obtain them.

- Let your boss know your career goals. Ask whether your goals are realistic, whether you have the skills to achieve your goals, and what training you should take to improve yourself.
- Develop action plans that are goal-oriented. Review the goals and minigoals regularly to see if you are on track. If you are not, evaluate your steps and adjust your plan accordingly.
- Find a mentor. Identify someone in the organization who is well regarded and whom you admire, someone who complements your skills and traits. When you are faced with difficult situations seek advice, or ask your mentor to evaluate your decisions.
- Project a "can do" approach. Don't burden others with problems, doubts, and roadblocks. Speak about opportunities and solutions, not problems.
- Always be positive; think of the glass as half full rather than half empty. Remember: More people are fired for poor attitudes than for any other reason.
- Focus your energy on jobs that will:
  - ✓ Best use your skills
  - ✓ Have the greatest chance of success
  - ✓ Require an optimal amount of effort and resources
- Do, and be seen to be doing, things that help your organization:
  - ✓ Pass on sales leads.
  - ✓ Look for and suggest ways to reduce costs.
  - ✓ Become a source of information. Keep up with news trends by scanning business and trade publications. Circulate materials to people who can benefit.
  - ✓ Undertake less popular assignments.
- If unpleasant news is on the way, let your boss know first and early. Nobody wants unpleasant surprises, particularly ones that might embarrass them.
- Know what your boss expects of you. If possible, agree on measurable goals so that your achievements are indisputable.
- Ask for more authority and autonomy. Stretch yourself. Take on more than you think you are capable of to prove to yourself, and others, what you can do.
- Compete against yourself and let others judge if you are better than your peers. Competing against your peers will

increase their resentment toward you. You will become the subject of sniping and back-stabbing.

- Be willing to accept criticism. The critique will be most effective if you do the following:
  - ✓ Control your emotions. Don't be defensive. Be objective.
  - ✓ Put yourself in the critic's place. Would you take a similar view?
  - ✓ Treat each criticism as an opportunity to learn and grow.
  - ✓ Defend yourself if, after reflection, you feel that your evaluation was unfair.
  - ✓ Thank the person giving the criticism, even if you disagree with the content.
- Learn from setbacks. You will get no benefit from blaming others or continuing to be angry. Find out what you did wrong. Try, as hard as it may be, to be objective. Above all, fix the problem and focus your energies on avoiding the same mistake.
- Acknowledge the help of others publicly. This will increase your network of supporters.
- Learn to get what you want, while still being liked. Don't alienate important people since you never know when they could be influential in picking the next person to be promoted.
- If you sense that a desirable job will be available in the foreseeable future, make yourself a leading contender by:
  - ✓ Taking on extra work to demonstrate your skill in that job
  - ✓ Letting the right people know of your interest
  - ✓ Updating the skills and knowledge required for the job

Career Planning

Progressing in your career requires that you set personal goals and find ways of adding value and developing skills that are easily portable.

The only person who can plan your career is you. In an environment where downsizing, reengineering, and reorganization are prevalent, opportunities for advancement are few and far between. Here is how you can improve your chances of enhancing your career:

- Keep yourself informed about new trends and ideas. You can do this by:
  ✓ Retaining membership in professional organizations
  ✓ Reading books and articles on your area of expertise
  ✓ Attending conferences, seminars, and workshops
- Promote yourself as a proponent of new ideas, so that you are seen as an agent of change rather than a dinosaur.
- Keep your mind open to change. Be prepared to run with new ideas. Volunteer for committees that will be studying new technologies.
- Keep your resumé updated. Include every successful project, particularly those that added value to your department's objectives in a measurable way. Highlight your greatest achievements. Don't be modest.
- Take advantage of any courses your organization offers. You will always learn something at each session. Add these to your resumé. Make sure that your boss knows what courses you are attending and how they are helping you.
- Expand your network of business associates. Keep in touch. Let them know what you are doing and where you are headed.
- Remember, it's not what you know that counts, it's who

you know! Keep in touch with people who are aware of employment opportunities both within and outside your organization. Put recruitment professionals high on your networking list.

- Evaluate your worth in the marketplace. This information will let you know if you are adequately paid or give you the motivation to seek justice inside or outside your firm.
  Your value can be determined by three factors:
  1. The need for what you do
  2. Your ability to do it
  3. How difficult it is to replace you
- Identify your strengths. Analyze the things you excel at. Confirm your evaluation with feedback from key people around you.
- Focus on the skills that help your organization in a way that no one else can. For example, polish up on a foreign language if your company is entering that market.

Career: What to Do if You Are Fired

If you aren't fired with enthusiasm, you will be fired with enthusiasm.

VINCE LOMBARDI

A s many companies continue to flatten their structure to become more effective and reduce costs, laying off managers is commonplace. If you are caught in the restructuring, make the best of a bad situation by doing the following.

At the Exit Interview

- Do not show anger or resort to blaming anyone. A collaborative but firm attitude will allow you to depart gracefully, with as much dignity and cash as possible.
- Don't sign any release or settlement documentation until it is fair and reasonable. If you are unsure, consult a labor lawyer. The guideline of one week's pay for every year of service is a start, but you may be able to negotiate for more (see "Negotiating").
- Seek outplacement services as part of your severance package. A counselling service can provide you with:
  ✓ Personality and skills assessment
  ✓ Resumé skills
  ✓ Interview coaching
  ✓ Contacts
  ✓ Guidance on a broad range of job search strategies
  A counsellor can help you come to terms with your situation, act as a sounding board for new ideas, and help you turn adversity into opportunity. If you are able to work out of an

outplacement service's office, you will be able to keep up a daily routine and make your transition less stressful.

Later

- Come to terms with your situation by sharing your pain with those closest to you. Releasing your anger and frustration verbally will enable you to refocus on the rest of your life.
- Develop a network of contacts. Go through your diaries and business cards and make a list of people to contact. You never know who can offer you a job, an idea, or a lead.
- Write a resumé that, while being accurate, will excite people with the possibility of employing you. Your resumé should be short, accurate, and pertinent. It should also:
  ✓ Focus on a specific job
  ✓ Highlight your strengths
  ✓ Appeal aesthetically
- Meet with people who have worked with you professionally. Seek their feedback on your strengths and weaknesses. Plan to deal with your shortcomings so that you will be even more valuable to your next employer than you were to the last.
- Fantasize about what you would love to do, irrespective of practical realities such as money or location. Find out about those jobs from people in the field, asking specifically how they got those jobs. Evaluate whether you have the time, patience, and confidence to make a career change.
- Set up a plan to get as many job offers as possible. Put aside time each day for:
  ✓ Reviewing and responding to newspaper advertisements
  ✓ Calling people in your network
  ✓ Sending out targeted broadcast letters
- Sharpen your interview skills. It would be a tragedy if you got an interview and then blew the opportunity to get a job offer (see page 16, "Things to Avoid in a Job Interview"). Practice with a counsellor or a confidant.

Change

The future isn't what it used to be.

We all know how hard change is, but adapting to change can be challenging and fun. Here's what you can do to ease the pain:

- Be optimistic about change. Look at it as an opportunity and a challenge rather than a threat.
- Anticipate change and its potential impact on your work area. Find out how significant it will be. Determine the following:
  ✓ Who will be affected?
  ✓ How significant is the change?
  ✓ Is the change organizational, legal, technological, or procedural?
  ✓ Is the change urgent?
- Evaluate your people's ability to absorb the change. Their adaptability may be influenced by previous experiences, their length of service, and your style of leadership.
- Whenever possible, give your associates advance notice of pending changes so that they have time to adjust. Rally your people to meet the challenge together.
- When you communicate change to those around you, describe it in the context of "the big picture." Show how the change will impact your corporate mission and goals.
- Explain how changes will affect each person. People are fearful of things that affect them directly: changing routine, losing jobs, or being moved to new areas. Be available to answer questions and listen to concerns.
- Prepare people by giving them the tools to master changes in processes or technology. Provide them with seminars,

hands-on experiences, and trips to companies that have made similar changes.
- Show people how they can benefit from change. If the task requires more effort, skill, or responsibility, provide rewards such as higher pay, more time off, or specialized training.
- Listen to your people's ideas on how to make change as smooth as possible. Their involvement will increase their commitment.
- Ask for new ideas soon after a change has been made so that you reinforce the fact that change is constant.

Dealing with Failure

- Some of your plans for change will fail. Treat failure as a learning experience. Analyze what you did wrong so that you don't make the same mistake again.
- If you have failed, don't give up. Get up, dust yourself off, and try again and again until you succeed.
- Let others benefit from your mistakes. Inform your peers of problems you encountered so that they can avoid the same pitfalls.
- Let your associates know that it is permissible to fail. However, encourage them to take responsibility for fixing their mistakes and learning from them.
- Set a time frame for analyzing and evaluating the results of your change.

Change: Evaluating Team Readiness

A sk your people to complete the following survey anony-mously. Collect the responses, analyze the data, and modify your implementation to suit your circumstances.

This survey will help us introduce change in our work area with the least disruption. Please help me by completing the survey and returning it in the enclosed envelope.

Signed _____

Mark an X in the chosen circle key: ① = strongly disagree; ② = disagree; ③ = neither agree or disagree; ④ = agree; ⑤ = strongly agree.

- Change usually creates more problems than solutions.   ①   ②   ③   ④   ⑤
- Before making changes, my boss asks my opinion.   ①   ②   ③   ④   ⑤
- Change is needed here.   ①   ②   ③   ④   ⑤
- I never hear about changes until afterwards.   ①   ②   ③   ④   ⑤
- When changes are made here, employees always seem to lose out.   ①   ②   ③   ④   ⑤
- I don't look forward to changes.   ①   ②   ③   ④   ⑤

Change: Overcoming Resistance

The science of today is the technology of tomorrow.

EDITH TELLER

Never assume that people will be as excited about a new idea as you are. People usually see obstacles before benefits. As a leader, you need to nurture acceptance as quickly and as painlessly as possible. Here are some useful ideas:

- Demonstrate your own commitment in meaningful ways. For example, show that you are investing resources in the new concept.
- Evaluate how committed people are. If there is resistance, find out why. Hold a meeting. Ask for reasons without criticizing or being defensive.
- When aware of the reasons, remove the problem. If the problem is misperception, show things as they really are, giving examples or illustrations. If the concern is lack of skills, offer training.
- Offer support and encouragement during the transition. Indicate your willingness to accept some level of imperfection and mistakes throughout the transition. This will reduce people's fears of failure.
- Give as much information as possible. Focus on information that will be relevant to your people.
- Involve people in identifying ways to demonstrate their commitment. The greater their involvement, the greater their commitment.
- Negotiate goals that can be used to evaluate people's commit-

ment. These should be specific, measurable, and realistic. Set a meeting to evaluate progress.

- Recognize the phases that most people experience during change:
  ✓ Denial
  ✓ Anger
  ✓ Acceptance
  ✓ Action

Make people aware of these phases, indicating that these reactions are normal. Help your people deal with the transition.

Chemical Abuse

Abuse of drugs and alcohol in the workplace is a monumental problem. And anyone can be an addict, from your CEO to your front-line worker. Here are practical ideas about what you can do:

- Communicate regularly with your people. Be aware of the following symptoms of abuse:
  - ✓ Excessive absenteeism, particularly on Mondays
  - ✓ Regular tardiness
  - ✓ Declining productivity
  - ✓ Increased injuries and accidents
  - ✓ Personal problems—legal, financial, or family
  - ✓ Constant and/or suspicious phone calls
  - ✓ Physical deterioration such as slurred speech, runny nose, scratching, and dry skin
  - ✓ Changes in interactions with others
  - ✓ Increased isolation from or conflict with peers
  - ✓ Rebellious behavior towards authority
  - ✓ Erratic behavior, mood swings, disorientation
  - ✓ Increased washroom visits
- When you think there's a problem, you should:
  - ✓ Prepare to deal with it assertively
  - ✓ Document signs and obvious patterns
- Never:
  - ✓ Enable the person to get away with poor job performance
  - ✓ Ignore or excuse unacceptable behavior
  - ✓ Take on the person's responsibilities

✓ Make excuses to others, cover up the problem, pick up the slack, or fill in for them

✓ Feel responsible

✓ Try to solve problems you are not qualified to solve

- Confront the person with your evidence. This should be done privately and in a supportive manner (see "Counselling"). In your discussion you should:

  ✓ Avoid blaming, using guilt tactics, or getting sidetracked with the associate's personal problems. Stick to work issues.

  ✓ Refer the associate to a professional to deal with personal problems. An employee assistance program is geared to deal with these issues.

  ✓ Clarify goals and standards. The person should refocus on what is expected of him or her.

  ✓ Let the person know the consequences of poor performance.

- If performance does not improve, follow disciplinary steps according to company policy.

  ✓ If you are unionized, enlist your union representative's support in your actions, be they disciplinary or focused on rehabilitation.

Coaching

Good coaches train their people to do the job right every time. While most coaching is done in technical areas of a job, you can also coach your people to improve their team and interpersonal skills.

- Meet daily with people—either collectively or one on one—to obtain agreement on what is expected of them.
- Use these methods to help your people reach their goals:
  ✓ **Mentoring.** Model the skills you expect others to use.
  ✓ **Counselling.** Help your associates find solutions through step-by-step self-discovery.
  ✓ **Training.** Increase your associates' skills by:
    — Explaining what you want them to do
    — Showing them how to do it
    — Letting them try, while you observe
    — Giving them feedback on their performance
  ✓ **Confronting.** Let your associates know when their behavior fails to meet agreed-upon standards.
- If associates fail to do the job right, redirect them. Show them again. Ask them to confirm their understanding of the task. Have them demonstrate their understanding by showing you how to do the task.
- If the task is large or appears difficult, break it into pieces. Learning one step at a time will build the trainee's self-confidence.
- If associates do not improve after a number of trials, determine whether the cause is attitudinal or a lack of aptitude. If it is the latter, move them to a job that better suits their skill

set. If it is attitudinal, determine the cause (see "Counselling") and solution. If this does not work—and only a small minority will not respond—go through the disciplinary procedure and terminate the individual.

- Give people regular feedback. Wherever possible, measure their performance so that they know when they are improving or getting worse.
- As people's skills improve, encourage them to discover new and better ways of doing things. Praise them for their new ideas.
- Allow people to improvise. Even if the new method does not fit your perception of the best method, encourage a spirit of enterprise.

Commitment

We fail or succeed together.
If we fail, no one is a winner.

BRENDA LAVIGNE

G aining commitment from one individual is difficult. Getting buy-in from your team is even more challenging. Here are some key strategies for success:

- Be clear about what it is that you need commitment to before speaking to your team. If it is not clear to you, don't jeopardize your credibility by presenting your confusion to the group.
- Arrange a meeting with your team. Explain your challenge to them and describe what a successful outcome will look like.
- Explain the benefits to be gained if the project or task is completed on time and on budget.
- Show empathy for reasonable concerns. Indicate your understanding of people's feelings.
- Gauge their buy-in to your proposal. Encourage them to speak up so that all issues are put on the table. Record these on a flipchart.
- Work through obstacles at your meetings. Offer solutions to the issues that you have control over. Ask for input regarding issues that your team can deal with.
- Involve the team in deciding how the goal and progress can be measured.
- Set a long-term goal. Get approval. Do the same for shorter-term goals.
- Ask individuals to identify their contribution to the goal. Ask what they expect of others.
- Confirm the commitment of each associate. Document all agreed upon actions in minutes of the meeting. Copy and circulate later.

Communicating Across Language Barriers

The most important thing in communication is to hear what isn't being said.

PETER F. DRUCKER

O ur workforce is becoming more diverse. Communicating with people for whom English is a new language is critical.

- Be patient. If you expect too much, too quickly, you will confuse and frustrate the people involved.
- Don't show anger if people don't understand at first.
- If people speak English poorly but understand reasonably well, ask them to demonstrate their understanding through actions rather than words.
- Avoid jokes. Your humor will not be understood. Worse still, it might be seen as a joke at their expense.
- Don't assume that difficulty understanding means lack of intelligence. Many people doing menial jobs in their adopted country were teachers, engineers, lawyers, and medical practitioners in their native countries.
- Speak slowly and clearly, but don't raise your voice.
- Use face-to-face communication whenever possible. Avoid telephone conversations.
- Break instructions into manageable steps.
- Use interpreters only if communications are impossible. Discourage people from becoming dependent on interpreters.
- Use pictures and diagrams instead of words. Back up verbal directions with simple written instructions.
- Encourage people to take English courses. Make time available for them to get to classes.

Communicating In Writing

Writing without thinking is like shooting without aiming.

ARNOLD GLASGOW

M ost people find it difficult to state their thoughts clearly on paper, resulting in ineffective communication. Here are some ways to improve:

- Think about what you need to communicate and why. Decide which method would be most effective: oral or written. Documentation is often preferable if:
  - ✓ A major decision is required
  - ✓ The issue is complex
  - ✓ The matter needs to be studied prior to a decision
- Your communication should follow a logical sequence:
  - ✓ Begin with the reason for the communication.
  - ✓ Next, state what is expected from each recipient.
  - ✓ Then provide pertinent information or decisions.
- Always be brief and specific: Focus on the steak, not the sizzle. The reader should not have to search for your key thoughts.
- Make your first paragraph short. Get your reader committed by making it look easy. Vary the length of subsequent paragraphs, keeping them brief, too.
- Don't clutter your writing with details. Use attachments for background information. Refer to the attachments in your document: "see Attachment A."
- Make sure people won't need a dictionary to understand you.
  - ✓ Don't repeat yourself.
- People who are sent copies should not be surprised to receive

the document. Your reasons for copying people should not be politically motivated.
- Keep examples of excellent writing to use as models.
- Avoid sexist descriptions or repeatedly using *he/she*. Here is how to overcome this problem:
  - ✓ Write sentences in the plural. For example, "A manager should prepare his meeting" can be changed to "Managers should prepare their meetings."
  - ✓ Use *we, us,* or *our.* For example, "No man should have to go through this" can become "We should not have to go through this."
  - ✓ Use nouns instead of pronouns. For example, "He who laughs last, laughs best" can be written as "The person who laughs last, laughs best."
  - ✓ Avoid pronouns if possible. For example, "The manager should tell his workers" could be changed to "The manager should tell workers."
- Avoid legalese. Use a conversational style of writing. Write as if you were talking to friends.
- If a sentence doesn't read well, repeat it aloud. Then repeat it again and again, making changes until it sounds right.

Communicating: Managing the Grapevine

Surveys show that most people get the information they need through the grapevine rather than official channels. Here's what you can do to reduce the impact of distorted information.

Avoiding Rumors

- Take the attitude that it is better to give too much information than too little.
- Hold regular briefings, which by definition should be short. They can be stand-up meetings in the office or a huddle on the factory floor. If you don't have new information, encourage questions, which may uncover rumors you are not aware of.
- Keep a flipchart in your work area. Write news on it regularly. Allow your people to record questions that they want to deal with at your meetings.
- Anticipate issues that might provoke negative gossip. Deal with them right away.

Dealing with Rumors

- Never deny or lie about the truth—your credibility will suffer, and trust between you and your people will be jeopardized. Often information reaches your people before you get it. Try to track down the source and establish whether the information is truth or fiction. When you have the facts, let people have them right away.
- Go to the source of the rumor. Find out if you or your team will be affected. Find ways to position yourself to take advantage of the situation. Develop a plan that will

demonstrate how you and your people could help to make the change successful.

- When you go to the source of a rumor, don't demand answers or put people on the spot. Make it easy for them to help you by asking questions that can be dealt with hypothetically. For example: "If, at some time in the future, there was a downsizing, which departments would be cut first?" Watch their body language when they answer in order to understand how they feel about the issue.
- Maintain a positive attitude. Take particular care to do good work, since deteriorating attitude and work will make you stick out like a sore thumb.
- Be open to change. Look at all the alternatives. Change brings opportunities. New directions should challenge and energize you.
- Watch for signs that rumors are becoming reality. Typically, senior managers will be:
  - ✓ Spending more time in meetings
  - ✓ Looking harassed
  - ✓ Whispering among themselves
  - ✓ Taking phone calls or holding discussions behind closed doors

Communicating Upwards

The most important sale in life is to sell yourself to yourself.

MAXWELL MALTZ

Communicating effectively with those who have a higher rank is not only an important part of your job, it is also important for your career.

- Always keep your boss informed, particularly if a problem is looming. Bosses want to be prepared. They want to look good and in control. If you embarrass them, it will come back to haunt you.
- Do not delay bad news. The grapevine will get to your boss before you do, robbing you of the opportunity to put your own slant on the issue.
- Make an appointment to meet with your boss when the issue becomes pressing. When doing so, state your objective and the time needed to cover the subject.
- Let management know the impact and importance of your information and advice.
- When presenting information, have backup material available. Written documentation will strengthen your ability to influence.
- Present your ideas concisely and clearly.
- Be confident of your facts and opinions. Speak with a firm voice. Your body language should reinforce your confidence; lean forward and maintain eye contact on critical issues.
- Focus on solutions rather than problems. Anyone can highlight problems. Show that you not only have the answers but are willing to take responsibility to resolve them.

- Choose your words with care. For example, saying "To be honest with you" might suggest that you have not been honest to this point. Avoid exaggeration. Say "I have important information for you" rather than "I have terrible news for you."
- When you think your boss is being unreasonable, do not respond with anger or avoidance. Cool down; explain how you feel and why. And always use *I*, not *you*. For example, "I don't think it's right" will go over a lot better than "You are wrong."
- If your boss criticizes you, learn from the feedback. If the feedback is not specific, ask how your boss would deal with the same situation.
- If you are unsure about how receptive your boss will be to an important new idea, run it by in writing first. This will enable you to:
  ✓ Deal comprehensively with the issue
  ✓ Give your boss time to review your proposal
- Follow the chain of command. Don't intentionally go around your boss. If you do, keep your boss informed.

Communicating Verbally

Sticks and stones may break our bones, but words will break our hearts.

Robert Fulghum

Communication has always been, is, and will continue to be the number one problem in organizations. As a person in a leadership role, you must clearly communicate your vision of the future, your performance expectations, and results.

- Be clear and specific about what you want.
- If you are not sure that the people you are speaking to have understood you, ask them to repeat your message in their own words.
- Observe people's response to your message. Most of what people think is not expressed verbally. Learn to read people's thoughts through their facial expressions and hand and foot gestures. Above all, look at their eyes for signs of confusion, disagreement, disbelief, resistance, or understanding (see page 42, "Reading Body Language").
- If there is background noise, speak loudly or move to a quieter area. Use gestures to reinforce your verbal communication, especially in noisy areas.
- In order to keep people's attention, modulate your voice. Suddenly speaking louder or softer, quickly or slowly, will increase interest in what you are saying; so will pausing before or after a key point.
- Maintain eye contact with people you are talking to. Bear in mind their cultural background. In some cultures, excessive eye contact is a sign of disrespect.
- Pay full attention to the other person. Avoid taking phone calls or allowing interruptions to distract you. Don't hold two conversations at the same time.

- When you communicate an important point, raise your voice slightly or begin to speak deliberately. Also, let your body language reflect the importance of what you are saying by leaning forward, opening your eyes wider, and using appropriate hand gestures.
- Begin conversations positively. If there is potential for conflict, start off with something you both agree on. Build on areas that you have in common to establish a positive atmosphere that will enable you to tackle more difficult issues.
- Avoid using *but* to join sentences. This word immediately puts people on the defensive. A better word to use is *and*.
- Use *I* messages. Using *you* will make people defensive.

READING BODY LANGUAGE

Here are some signs that let you know what people are thinking or feeling:

- Crossed legs and arms   Not open to your ideas.
- Darting eyes   Anxious or lacking confidence.
- Eyes up at top left   Figuring a way to out-maneuver you. May be lying.
- Eyes up at top right   Wondering, trying to figure something out. Mental problem solving.
- Hands on hip or hip jutted out   Confident, almost arrogant, challenging.
- Jacket buttoned up   Formal.
- Jacket unbuttoned   Open, informal.
- Leaning back, arms behind head   Contemplating, skeptical.
- Looking over bifocals   Evaluative, skeptical.
- Open hands, palms down   Demanding.
- Open hands, palms up   Wanting, needing.
- Slouch   Low self-esteem.
- Slow blink   Don't enjoy being there.
- Smile   Enjoyment, pleasure.

Communicating With Associates

A well-informed employee is the best salesperson a
company can have.

E. J. Thomas

Employees value the opportunity to influence their company, to have their voices heard and to see changes as a
result of their input. Here is how you can encourage upward
communication:

- Encourage communication from your people. Manage by
  walking around. Be visible. Make it easy for associates to
  meet with you. Maintain an open-door policy.
- Listen to what associates are telling you. Listen to understand rather than to rebut. Listen to their thoughts as well as
  their feelings.
- Ask for associates' opinions. This gesture makes employees
  feel valued and can have a positive impact on their commitment.
- Encourage associates' ideas by setting up suggestion systems, performance improvement teams, focus groups, and
  communication sessions.
- Act on these ideas, to encourage involvement. If you can't
  act, explain as soon as possible.
- Thank associates for their suggestions, even if you don't
  always agree with them. Challenge yourself to think of how
  the idea could work rather than why it might not.
- Try smaller ideas. What associates could learn from a mistake
  will probably more than pay for the cost.
- Communicate in simple language. Don't confuse people by
  using vocabulary they are unlikely to understand.

- Demonstrate respect for your associates by showing interest in their ideas, listening to them, and encouraging their input.
- If you are not quite sure of an idea you are listening to, repeat it in your own words. This will reinforce your understanding and demonstrate your interest.
- Don't just tell your associates what to do; tell them why.
- Choose your words carefully. Associates may react strongly to words that put them down.
- Give bad news in private; one-on-one meetings (preferably in an informal atmosphere) make things appear less severe. In addition, such meetings provide an opportunity for your associate to vent frustrations, and the meetings enhance problem solving.
- Be conscious of your communication style. You will discourage communication if you:
  ✓ **Preach.** Talking in moralizing terms implies that others don't have the same or equal ethical standards.
  ✓ **Patronize.** It makes them feel like they are being treated like a child.
  ✓ **Scold.** Waving your finger at someone makes them feel inferior. Focus on the behavior or problem.
  ✓ **Are negative.** Don't prejudice ideas. Look for the positive. If you always show your associates what's wrong with their suggestions, they soon stop giving them.
- Maintain a positive approach. Smile. Look and act interested.
- Don't try to become popular with your associates by criticizing your boss. You can't develop trust if you can't be trusted.
- Don't voice disagreement with your boss's instructions to your associates. Voice them to your boss.
- If your associates are angry:
  ✓ Don't get into an argument. It will escalate the problem.
  ✓ Listen to them without interruption. Allowing them to let off steam will solve half the problem.
  ✓ Recognize their right to feel angry.
  ✓ Ask them for ideas on how to solve the problem.

Conflict Between Associates

It's better to debate a question without settling it, than to settle a question without debating it.

JOSEPH JOUBERT

Conflict about ideas can promote creativity and innovation, but conflict between people leads to high stress, poor morale, and low productivity.

- Assess:
  - ✓ The seriousness of the conflict
  - ✓ People's ability to solve the conflict on their own
- If the problem is not serious, do nothing.
- Encourage individuals to resolve the matter on their own. Follow up. If the matter has been dealt with adequately, praise parties.
- If the problem is complex, encourage parties to:
  - ✓ Listen
  - ✓ Try to see the issue from the other's point of view
  - ✓ Focus on common interests rather than differences
- If the problem is disruptive and the parties do not have the ability to solve the conflict on their own, set up a meeting to mediate the conflict with both people present.
- Before the meeting, determine whether the issues are real or merely perceptions. Real issues are based on facts, whereas perceptions are influenced by people's intuition.

At a Mediation Meeting

- At the start, present the background to the meeting and establish a goal that you want each person to strive towards.

- Next, establish ground rules. Ask people to:
  - ✓ Respect others' ideas
  - ✓ Try to see the problem from the other's viewpoint
  - ✓ Focus on the problem, not the person
  - ✓ Work towards a solution
- State the consequences if the problem is not solved. Don't threaten the combatants.
- Use humor appropriately. For instance, you can exaggerate the situation to minimize the reality.
- Ask individuals to state their position. Summarize your understanding. Help people separate critical from noncritical issues. List the key issues for each person on a flipchart so that they can be reviewed more objectively.
- Prioritize the problems by dealing with critical issues first. By considering one issue at a time, from each person's list, find the cause of the problem. Invite suggestions. If none are forthcoming, suggest ideas to get the ball rolling. Confirm and summarize causes.
- Move to solutions. Ask each person to take responsibility for solving problems. Ask for specific solutions and for the dates by which they will be carried out.
- Summarize the meeting so people are clear about what was discussed and how matters are to be resolved. Next, thank them for their help, and praise them (if appropriate) for their risk taking and openness.

After Mediation

- Set a meeting to review progress. If things are better, praise the parties again and assure them of your continued support and interest. If little progress has been made, find out why and continue working to find an amicable solution.
- If one of the parties continues to obstruct resolution of the problem, and performance is being affected, you should begin the disciplinary process.

Conflict between You And Others

If your neighbor does you some harm, do not pretend you are still friends . . . do not hate him but reprove him for what he did and through this peace can be reestablished.

RASHBAM, BIBLICAL SCHOLAR

Conflict is stressful. It undermines your ability to work with people and makes it harder for everyone concerned to achieve their objectives. Here are some things you can do to resolve issues.

When Conflict Occurs

- Deal with conflict right away so that the problem doesn't mushroom.
- Ask the person to set a time to resolve your differences together. Accommodate them if the present is inopportune.
- Set a meeting in a private place.

At Your Meeting

- Establish the climate for a good interchange. Be constructive and positive in your words and body language. Point out that the conflict is not good for either of you and that you are determined to resolve it.
- Make the point that there are two sides to every story and that you are probably the source of the problem, too.
- State your case. Be firm and clear. Maintain eye contact.

- Be specific about the things that bother you. Give examples. Don't exaggerate or stretch the truth.
- Don't use inflammatory language. If you do, the person will focus on your words rather than on resolving the problem.
- Take ownership for the problem. Use *I* whenever possible instead of *you*. "I feel angry" or "I am annoyed" is better than "You did this wrong." Using *you* will tend to make the other person defensive.
- Don't go over long-gone events. Stick to current events.
- Listen carefully to the other person's case. Do not interrupt. While you may not agree with everything, look for areas of agreement. Be objective. Nod or confirm legitimate points.
- Summarize the other person's points to show that you understand. Show empathy. A statement such as "I would feel like that, too" will go a long way to reducing the anger, so that you can both get on with solving the problem.
- Once you both agree on the problem and causes, move to solutions. Offer ideas about what you will do to address the other person's concerns. Ask what that individual will do to address your issues. Involving your associate in problem solving will increase commitment to resolving the problem.
- Agree to disagree where no resolution can be found. Indicate your respect for the other person's position even if you do not agree with it.
- Conclude the meeting with:
  ✓ A summary of your discussions and commitments
  ✓ A statement of your appreciation for the other person's willingness to resolve your differences

After the Meeting

- Be mindful of the issues raised at your meeting. Live up to your commitments. Express your appreciation if others live up to theirs.

Conflict Prevention

A fault is a crack gradually widening and separating people.

CARL JUNG

Conflict is a natural consequence of teamwork. Conflict is healthy when people challenge the status quo or debate how better to serve the customer. However, when the conflict stems from individuals challenging each other, it can be unhealthy. Here is how you can reduce interpersonal conflict:

- Focus on facts and information rather than rumors and feelings.
- Involve people in changes that you make. Listen to and understand their interests, objectives, and concerns.
- Keep communication open and objective to reduce potential suspicion and hostility.
- Deal with issues that are hard to discuss, otherwise the problem will intensify.
- Resolve immediately issues that prevent completion of obligations by the targeted date.
- Encourage conflict between your associates that relates to ideas. Discourage interpersonal conflict.
- Ensure that your people understand how conflict will be dealt with when it arises.
- Keep your ear to the ground. Tap into the grapevine so that you can identify issues before they get blown out of proportion. Deal with these issues before they become disruptive.
- Establish ground rules for your team. For example, members don't have to like each other, but they should respect each other.

Counselling

Sometimes employees' personal problems interfere with their job performance. If this occurs, a manager must step in to address the problem.

Preparation for Counselling

- Collect the facts. Data will be more useful than opinions. Note how much performance has declined.
- Set clear objectives. Know what you want to achieve when the process is over.
- Make notes about what you intend to say. Rehearse your introduction to ensure a smooth start to the meeting.
- Schedule an appointment to meet. Set aside at least 30 minutes for the interview.
- Meet in a neutral office or meeting room. Privacy is essential.
- Organize the furniture to promote a problem-solving atmosphere. Sit next to the associate.
- Plan to take notes of agreements and action plans.

During the Interview

- Greet employees warmly, but don't try to soften them with praise that is unrelated to the discussion. The faster you get down to dealing with the issue the better.
- Describe the problem. Give examples.
- Encourage your associate to help find the cause of the problem. Ask open-ended questions such as:
  ✓ Do you have any idea why that happens?
  ✓ What do you think is the problem?
- Listen empathetically. Show your support and confidence in the associate's ability to solve the problem.
- If the person is reluctant to discuss the problem, ask if the

problem concerns personal matters. If so, you have two options:

1. If the person is comfortable discussing the matter with you and is confident in your ability to assist, take a problem-solving approach: Encourage the employee to identify the problem, its primary cause, and possible solutions. It's important to have the employee resolve the issue to develop problem-solving skills and buy into the solution. Arrange a follow-up meeting at which you can monitor progress and show your continued interest in the matter.
2. If the person is not comfortable discussing personal matters, ask if professional help is an option. If acceptable, obtain counselling quickly. Follow up as needed to assure your support and continued interest.

- If your associate refuses to discuss the problem, and the problem is affecting performance, you will have to surmise the cause and identify your own solutions.
- When you establish the cause, ask what the associate will do about it. If there is more than one solution, make a list. Have the associate evaluate each solution.
- Don't take responsibility for solving the problem. Your associate must make the decisions. Ask for a commitment within a definite time period.
- Summarize your discussion to avoid future uncertainty.

After the Interview

- Follow up to ensure that agreed upon actions have been taken. Show appreciation for positive change. If no change has occurred, repeat the procedure, emphasizing consequences if improvement does not take place. Consequences might include:
  ✓ A note in the file
  ✓ Time off without pay
  ✓ Termination

Creativity

The reasonable man adapts himself to the world. The unreasonable man persists in trying to adapt the world to himself. Therefore, all progress depends on the unreasonable man.

GEORGE BERNARD SHAW

As a manager, you must ensure that your associates are given the opportunity to contribute new, innovative solutions. The following strategies will help you:

- Look for creative people. They:
  - ✓ May be unconventional (in their approach, dress, etc.)
  - ✓ Often appear as troublemakers
  - ✓ Are persistent
  - ✓ Are willing to take risks
  - ✓ Have vivid imaginations
- Encourage your creative people to take risks by rewarding efforts and process, not only results. Doing so sends a clear message that the action is as important as the outcome.
- Accept small improvements rather than expecting major ones; base hits are important since they prepare people to strive for home runs later on.
- Set up a budget for experimentation to show your interest in new initiatives.
- Allow mistakes. It's impossible to make significant improvements without errors. Don't look at failure as the end of the road. Rather, consider it a stepping stone. Involve your people in finding out what went wrong and how obstacles can be overcome.
- Support persistence. Not all innovations come from flashes of imagination. Sometimes real innovations come from hours, days, and even years of trial and error.

- Be open and responsive to new ideas. Listen to be influenced rather than concentrating on developing a rebuttal.
- If you find it difficult to assess the merits of a new idea, find someone who can and who might advocate on behalf of the idea.
- Maintain a relaxed atmosphere. Having fun creates a playful environment that encourages creative actions.
- Encourage foolish or impractical ideas, particularly those that don't have an immediate negative influence on your business. These ideas can often be built on and can lead to new innovations.
- Challenge people to come up with new ideas daily.
- Leave a flipchart in the work area. Encourage people to record ideas as they occur. Share and evaluate these ideas with your people at your next meeting.
- Go outside of your business to look for new ideas that could work in your area. While you may get ideas from similar work areas within your organization, you will find more innovative solutions in other organizations and industries.
- Challenge yourself and your workers to think of more reasons why a new idea would work, rather than reasons why it would not.
- Increase the value of your ideas by applying the SCAMPER process:
  Substitute
  Combine
  Adapt, add to, adjust
  Modify, magnify, minify
  Put pieces to other uses
  Expand, eliminate, elaborate
  Reverse, rearrange

The Scamper Process*

- **Substitute** similar items to form new products.
  - ✓ Lollipops for cotton swabs
  - ✓ Plastic for metal
- **Combine** distinctly different items to produce a synergistic product or service.
  - ✓ Carpark and building
  - ✓ Helium and engine to make a blimp
- **Adopt, add, or adjust** similar items.
  - ✓ Two blades to make a twin-blade shaving system
- **Modify, magnify, or minify** for other uses.
  - ✓ Compact discs
- **Put** pieces to other uses.
  - ✓ A newspaper for packing
- **Eliminate** unnecessary elements.
  - ✓ Eliminate packaging by using refills
- **Reverse** or rearrange items.
  - ✓ A knife can become a chopper

*The examples are product based, but SCAMPER can be used in all types of problem-solving situations.

Customer Service

The most important raison d'être for you and your people should be to provide superb service quickly and in a cost effective manner.

- Constantly make your people aware of the importance of meeting customers' needs. Customer issues should be emphasized in department meetings, in informal discussions, and on your bulletin board.
- Invite customers into your work area. Let them provide feedback on service.
- In order to remind employees about the importance of customers, place notes and posters on walls and bulletin boards. Display your mission statement, which describes:
  ✓ What you do
  ✓ For whom
  ✓ Where (geographic area)
  ✓ How you serve customers (quality, responsiveness, caring, value)
  ✓ Why you do what you do
- Measure critical indicators of customer satisfaction such as delivery, service, and quality. Display these measures where everyone can see them. Explain the link between the mission and the measures so that people can see how they are related.
- Involve your people in the collection of data on customer service. This will help them develop ownership and responsibility for performance.
- Obtain formal feedback from your customers through written

or person-to-person surveys. Analyze the data. Prioritize opportunities. Involve your people in suggesting and implementing changes.

- Your best guarantee of good service is happy employees. Maintain high morale by creating a positive environment. People will respond positively if you:
  - ✓ Listen to them
  - ✓ Keep them informed
  - ✓ Acknowledge them for above average performance
- In a nutshell, treat people as you would want to be treated.
- Keep your people informed about minimum customer service standards. Your associates should know why these standards are important and should be trained to attain them.
- When customer service improves, immediately praise your people. Conversely, when performance declines, make your team aware of the change. Seek their ideas about how to improve performance.
- Although not all customer services are easy to measure, show your appreciation when you observe your people:
  - ✓ Working hard to solve a problem
  - ✓ Being particularly courteous
  - ✓ Going the extra mile
- Make customer service a key element of your performance appraisal system. Involve your people in setting their own goals.
- Improve customer service by teaching your people skills such as:
  - ✓ How to handle difficult customers
  - ✓ Listening
  - ✓ Knowing what customers want
  - ✓ Problem solving
  - ✓ Telephone skills
- Give your people the power to solve customer problems. As they exercise this responsibility wisely, expand their level of authority.
- Constantly ensure that your people have the power to make decisions. Give your people training with guidelines so that they can deal with problems quickly.
- Encourage your people to treat angry customers with empa-

thy. Viewing the situation from the customer's perspective will increase enthusiasm to deal with problems without focusing on the customer's behavior.

- Encourage and reward change. Celebrate small successes. Strive for base hits rather than home runs. Large gains will result from many small improvements, and the size of improvements will increase as your people's confidence grows.
- Always make customer service a priority. Show leadership by dropping everything when a customer problem occurs.
- Evaluate every step in your process to determine whether or not it adds value to your customer. Cut out or reduce waste. This will reduce your delivery time dramatically.
- Don't let untrained personnel deal with complex customer issues. Give them training and guidance before they mess up.
- Show you care by providing your home phone number to customers. Let them know that you do not consider it an imposition if they call for help outside of business hours.
- Compare yourself with departments and organizations doing similar activities to your own. The more different the organization is from your own, the more you will learn. This process, known as benchmarking (see page 12), will allow you to compare measurable performance and procedures.
- Don't implement ideas from the outside without adapting them to suit your environment.

Customer Focus Survey

Answer the following questions to determine how customer-focused you are.

	Yes	No
• Have you empowered your people to deal with most customer problems without having to refer to a higher authority?	❑	❑
• Do you invite customers to your departmental meetings to give you feedback on your performance?	❑	❑

- Do you have a formal system for tracking   ❏   ❏
  customer complaints?
- Do you measure critical indicators of   ❏   ❏
  customer satisfaction?
- Do you share statistics on customer service ❏   ❏
  levels with your people?
- Do you meet regularly with your people to   ❏   ❏
  continuously challenge yourself to improve
  levels of customer service?
- Do you recognize and reward outstanding   ❏   ❏
  customer service?
- Are customer service goals a part of your
  performance appraisal system? Do you
  enable and encourage your people to visit
  customers?

If you answered NO to any of these questions, you have room
for improvement.

Decision Making

Nothing is more difficult, and therefore more precious, than to be able to decide.

NAPOLEON BONAPARTE

How decisions are made has a lot to do with how effective the decisions turn out to be.

- Recognize that there are many ways to make decisions. Most commonly, decisions can be made by:
  - ✓ One person or a few people (minority)
  - ✓ Most people (majority)
  - ✓ With everyone's support (consensus)
- Learn which decision-making methods are appropriate for each situation.
- Minority decisions can take place when:
  - ✓ There is lack of time
  - ✓ There is an emergency
  - ✓ The issue relates to health and safety
  - ✓ The decision is strategic
  - ✓ One person is the acknowledged expert
- The majority opinion should be used to make decisions when:
  - ✓ A decision is required quickly
  - ✓ There are too many people to negotiate a consensus
  - ✓ The issue is very divisive
- Decisions that impact your associates and require their commitment should be made by consensus.
- If you want your team to reach a consensus, let them know the place and time for the meeting in advance. With a few days notice they will have time to consider alternative ideas and arrive at the meeting with an informed choice.
- At your meeting, you can reach consensus quickly using the

Nominal Group Technique. This process consists of eight critical steps:

1. **Set a goal.** "We want to reach consensus on _____."
2. **Agree on the process.** Ask participants if they will support the majority. Any other constraints should also be agreed to.
3. **Generate ideas silently.** Participants record their ideas.
4. **Collect ideas by round-robin.** Each member gives one idea in turn. These ideas are recorded without discussion.
5. **Clarify ideas.** Key ideas are evaluated in greater detail. If you have a long list, vote to establish the top five. Next, spend time evaluating each idea by looking at pros and cons.
6. **Take a vote.** Participants make their choices: for example, first choice gets 5 points, second choice gets 3 points, third choice gets 1 point. Alternatively, members can vote on all items they consider significant.
7. **Tally the votes.** The leader counts the votes for each idea and identifies the top choice(s).
8. **Check for consensus.** The leader checks to see if everyone either agrees with the majority or, at least, supports the most popular choice.

- If you cannot reach a consensus, your options are to:
  - ✓ Tell people what your decision will be if no consensus is reached
  - ✓ Ask people to listen to one another and be accommodating
  - ✓ Review each person's position by canvassing them, one at a time
- If rigidity persists, you should make the decision. Generally, people will find this acceptable since they did have a choice to reach a consensus first.
- For more complex decisions use a matrix or tally sheet (see Figure 1).

Figure 1. Decision making matrix.

ITEM	IMPORTANCE	COST	EASE OF IMPLEMENTATION	VALUE TO CUSTOMER	OTHER	TOTAL
NOTE: Score 1 to 5 for each item, in each column; 1 = worst, 5 = best.						

- Allow each person to evaluate each idea by ranking it in terms of the agreed-to criteria. Collect the sheets and create a master tally sheet.
- Use the tally sheet for Step 6 of the Nominal Group Technique. It is important that people agree in advance to support the majority, and that they confirm their support when the most popular choice is revealed.

Delegating

The highest manifestation of life is this: that a being governs its own actions. A thing which is always subject to the direction of another is somewhat of a dead thing.

St. Thomas Aquinas

A s a leader, you will be judged as much by what happens when you are present as by what happens when you are absent.

Good managers never put off till tomorrow what they can delegate today. A major cause of stress and poor time management is an unwillingness, or inability, to delegate responsibility to people who work for us. Delegating responsibility to others allows you to concentrate on your duties as manager: planning, problem solving, and other proactive matters. Failure to delegate forces you to spend too much time on trivial issues and to neglect critical opportunities. Here's what you can do to correct the situation.

General

- Write down all your activities for one week. Categorize them as A and B activities. All or most A activities can be delegated, including:
  - ✓ Routine work
  - ✓ Data collection
  - ✓ Attending meetings unrelated to adding value for internal or external clients

  You will be left with more enriching tasks, the B activities, that will use your conceptual and communication abilities, including:

✓ Strategic planning
✓ Coaching
✓ Goal setting
✓ Updating your people
✓ Problem solving
✓ Liaising with customers
✓ Carrying messages between those above and below you
- Accept that you cannot do everything, be everywhere, and make all decisions. Believe that your people are capable of doing more of your mundane work without much difficulty.
- Identify people who could take some of the load off your shoulders. These people:
  ✓ Have an interest in the job
  ✓ Have or will make the time to do jobs you delegate
  ✓ Have the skills to do the jobs
- If people have the time and inclination but not the skills, train them.

Delegation Meeting

- Set up a meeting (formal or informal depending on the circumstances). At the meeting, address the following:
  ✓ Explain the purpose.
  ✓ Describe the task you want done.
  ✓ Be specific about the goal.
  ✓ Stress how important it is that the task is done in a timely and accurate manner.
  ✓ Obtain agreement about the goal.
  ✓ Agree on a date by which the task will be completed.
  ✓ If the task is big, establish minigoals with corresponding time lines.
  ✓ Discuss benefits that people might enjoy as a result of taking on the new job. These might include increased responsibility, learning opportunities, added exposure in the organization, or promotion opportunities.
  ✓ Make sure that the person accepts the task and its scope. A handshake is an acceptable way of acknowledging acceptance.

- Assign responsibility and authority. Tell your associates how confident you are in their ability to do the job.
- Ask if the associate foresees any problems in achieving the task. Help to resolve any problems.

Later

- Monitor people as needed to ensure directions are clearly understood.
- Monitor performance closely at first and then less frequently. If associates are performing well, let them know. If not, give them appropriate feedback, focusing on the behavior, not the person.
- Show confidence in people by giving them some freedom to do the task their way.
- Ensure that people who work with you and your associate know that you have delegated the task and that you have given the associate the authority to do the job.

Discipline Interview

The superior man always remembers how he was punished for his mistakes. The inferior man always remembers what presents he got.

CONFUCIUS

The discipline interview is one of the most frequently avoided responsibilities of a manager because it brings to a head performance problems that, if not resolved, could lead to suspension or even termination. Here's how you can handle this difficult situation.

Before the Interview

- Prepare yourself thoroughly. Your files should contain documentation detailing specific performance problems, with dates, and a record of previous counselling sessions.
- Keep copies of any written warnings. Include dates, times, and rules broken or policies violated.
- In a unionized workplace environment, make sure that you abide by the terms of the collective agreement. If you are not sure of your rights, consult your labor relations expert.
- Invite the employee to a private place for the interview, preferably in neutral territory. In some instances, you may also want to include a recorder. If necessary, ensure that the shop steward is present.

During the Interview

- Get right to the point by explaining the reason for the interview.

- Be specific when describing the problem. Give examples, with dates.
- Ask if the employee shares your observation and concern. The more specifically you have described the problem, the more likely it is the employee will agree with you.
- Give your associate the opportunity to explain, and listen carefully.
- Let the associate know what stage in the disciplinary process has been reached: for example, first verbal warning or second written warning. State that the warning will be in the person's personnel file and how long it will remain there.
- Discuss the consequences if the problem continues. Again ask for confirmation of understanding.
- If suspension or termination is the next step, it should be noted in the last written report. For example, "If this poor performance occurs again, you will be suspended without pay for a period of X days."
- Summarize the meeting to avoid ambiguity or misunderstanding.
- Establish a follow-up meeting at which the associate's performance will be reevaluated.

Diversity

> The most practical advice for leaders is not to treat pawns like pawns, nor princes like princes, but all persons like persons.
>
> JAMES MACGREGOR BURNS

A n increasing percentage of our workers come from different countries, cultures, and backgrounds. The more we learn about, understand, and become sensitive to the differences, the better we are able to motivate people. People are motivated by unique and respectful treatment. Here are some guidelines for managing diversity:

- Use terminology that is not offensive when referring to race or ethno-cultural background.
- If possible, establish a buddy system for people with similar backgrounds, at least until they establish themselves in the social fabric of the organization.
- In order to understand people better, find out about their ethno-cultural backgrounds. This information will help you understand the individual's:
  - ✓ Greetings
  - ✓ Comfort with physical closeness
  - ✓ Tolerance for particular gestures
  - ✓ General attitudes towards authority and the opposite sex
  - ✓ Preferences in regard to different personality traits
  - ✓ Perceptions of time and punctuality
  - ✓ Attitudes towards other nationalities
  - ✓ Sense of humor
  - ✓ Emotions
  - ✓ Perceptions of status (for example, the value placed on particular possessions or achievements)
- If you find that people have a different sense of urgency from

yours, point out the difference and be prepared to negotiate a solution that will be mutually acceptable.

- Be mindful of different people's comfort with physical closeness. A particular distance may be perceived as a violation of personal space by one person and as acceptable by another. Be careful when touching. A light tap on the shoulder may be acceptable in one culture and offensive in another.
- Discover each person's unique communication system. Some people find directness to be rude. Others find complaining or indicating a lack of understanding to be humiliating.
- Never allow racial slurs to go unchecked in your work area. If you do nothing, you are condoning the behavior. People should understand that any stereotypical comments are offensive and unacceptable.
- Encourage social events at which your people can get to know one another.
- Use humor to create an atmosphere of harmony among workers. Laughing at yourself will show that you are only human, thereby giving your associates confidence when confronting you. However, racial jabs are a no-no.
- Understand that humor is used differently in different cultures. A wry sense of humor might be seen as fun in one culture but a personal affront in another.
- Find out how long people have been in your country. This information may indicate their knowledge of local customs.
- Recruit, promote, select, and train people from minority groups so that they are represented in all parts and levels of your organization. Give them responsibility and authority.
- Spend more time with people of different backgrounds in order to get to know them better.
- Become aware of your body language when dealing with minorities to avoid mistaken perceptions of prejudice.
- Expect problems between visible minorities, and prepare to deal with them. Never sweep racial problems under the carpet.
- Look for opportunities to adjust work to meet your people's needs rather than always waiting for people to adjust to the job.

MONOCHRONIC VS. POLYCHRONIC CULTURES*

Some of the values and customs of people who come from North American and northern and western European countries (monochronic) are different from those of people who come from other European, African, and Middle Eastern countries (polychronic). If you understand and accept the differences, you can work effectively with both groups, whatever your own background.

	Monochronic	Polychronic
Focus	One thing at a time Single-task dedication	Variety of things at once Easily distractible
Time	Concerned with precision (e.g., 5:30 P.M.)	Interest in general time (e.g., after work)
Punctuality	Sacred	Not sacred
Career	Me first	Us first
Plans	Follow steps religiously	Flexible
Privacy	Want individual space	Happy to share and be close to others
Sharing	Want to own tools Do not want to lend or borrow	Will share tools Happy to lend or borrow
Relationships	Short-term focus	Enduring
Pace	Hectic	Relaxed
Attitudes	Rigid	Flexible
Orientation	Task completion	People satisfaction

* The generalizations expressed here should not be taken literally since there are variations within each category.

Empowering

A candle loses nothing of its light by lighting another candle.

JAMES KELLER

You will get the most out of people if you treat them as partners and give them increasing power as their abilities improve.

- Accept the fact that you are fallible. Learn from others, particularly from someone who does the job regularly.
- Concern yourself with the process your people are using as well as the outcome.
- Allow people to discover their own ways to achieve goals.
- Encourage people to take responsibility for their decisions by giving them an opportunity to self-correct and learn from their mistakes.
- Establish clear boundaries. Be prepared to enlarge these boundaries as confidence and competence grow.
- Review your management systems regularly to ensure that they support rather than obstruct performance.
- Train your people continuously. This will increase their skills and confidence.
- Develop and nurture personal relationships based on respect, inclusion, and trust. Treat others as you want to be treated.
- Be patient and do not become discouraged if people don't jump at the first opportunity to take on new challenges. They may be suspicious of your motives—with good reason.
- Walk your talk! Consistent, supportive behavior will eventually help overcome your people's suspicions. Then they will jump at the opportunities you provide.

Exit Interview

Conducting an interview with an employee leaving the company can be a valuable management practice: What you learn can turn a problem into an opportunity.

Before the Interview

- Inform the exiting employee of your desire to collect information that could help improve working conditions.
- Ask if the associate prefers talking with you or someone else, such as a human resources person.
- Ask the associate to discuss any issues that would be useful to you as a manager. Say that you will treat all information confidentially.
- Schedule the meeting during the last week of the person's employment.

During the Interview

- Hold the interview in a neutral place. Your office may be intimidating. Consider having an exit luncheon for someone who has been a valued employee.
- Arrange the physical layout to promote a problem-solving discussion rather than a boss-subordinate interview. Sit next to the associate rather than opposite him or her.
- Listen without being defensive. Record the details.
- Get as much information as possible by covering:
  - ✓ Your perception of your own leadership and interaction with others in the department
  - ✓ Any job difficulties you were not aware of
  - ✓ Things the person enjoyed about the job
  - ✓ Any corporate policies and procedures that prevented the person from doing the job effectively or caused annoyance
  - ✓ Any other information the person feels you should know

- If the associate is vague, prod with specific open-ended questions. For example, "Could you give me an example of that?"
- Find out about the associate's new job. This information could give you ideas about what is wrong now. You might ask:
  ✓ What attracted the individual to the job
  ✓ How the new work environment will differ
  ✓ How salary and benefits compare

After the Interview

- Collate your information. Pass on important data to those who can take corrective action. Reflect on and then fix those things that you have control over.
- If the information gathered has been contentious, consider conducting a follow-up interview by phone or in person. Better still, consider having someone else do the interview if you feel that this will enhance the objectivity of information gathering. You may find that the person's perspective has changed once outside the organization.

EXIT INTERVIEW QUESTIONS
✓ If you had my job, what would you change first? Why?
✓ How could I improve our work area?
✓ What frustrated you most about the job?
✓ What did you like best about the job?
✓ What corporate policies do you feel are most praise-worthy?
✓ What corporate policies and procedures made your work life difficult? Why?
✓ What will your new job give you that we have not?
✓ What will you miss most about working here?
✓ If you could tell the president one thing, what would it be?
✓ What should we be doing to ensure that your replacement stays with us?

Feedback

> Do not reprove him in such a way that you bring sin upon yourself, such as by shaming him through reproving him in public.
>
> A. S. Hartom

One of a manager's most difficult skills is handling problem behavior. So we often avoid dealing with the problem, thereby condoning the behavior. Often, attempts to deal with performance are unsatisfactory: We attack the individuals, jeopardizing our relationship with them and damaging their self-esteem. The following guidelines will help you:

- Give the feedback as soon after the problem occurs as possible.
- Get an invitation. Ask the person when it is convenient to meet. This will get buy-in to the process. In the unlikely event that the employee refuses, you will need to be more assertive.
- Give the feedback in private. Allowing other people to see and hear the discussion will embarrass your associate.
- Don't beat around the bush. Tell the employee exactly what you have observed without diluting your thoughts into generalities. If possible, give dates and places. This will confirm that you have done your homework and are well prepared.
- Be sure that your associate knows the institution's goals and standards. If not, repeat them so that they are clearly understood.
- Focus on the problem, not on the person. Fix the problem without disrupting the employee's feelings of self-worth or putting the employee on the defensive. For example, saying "There is a 10 percent decline in your productivity" is better than saying "Your performance is worse than it was."
- Deal with issues your associate can control.

- Use *I* statements. Avoid conflict caused by using the word *you*. For example, "I get upset" is preferable to "You upset me."
- Involve the person. Although you should be armed with some solutions, the employee should be encouraged to participate in problem solving. Ask open-ended questions or allow the person to steer the conversation; after all, since the employee must implement the change, a commitment is essential.
- Choose your words carefully. Don't use inflammatory language because the person will focus on the way feedback is being given rather than on the message.
- Focus on solutions. Remember, you are giving feedback to correct a problem, not to browbeat the person.
- Check and clarify key discussion points so that there will be no misunderstanding.
- Summarize the discussion at the end so that you both clearly understand what was said and what was agreed upon.
- Arrange for a follow-up meeting at which time you will both review progress.
- Help yourself by following a systematic feedback process, as shown on the next page.

FEEDBACK ROAD MAP

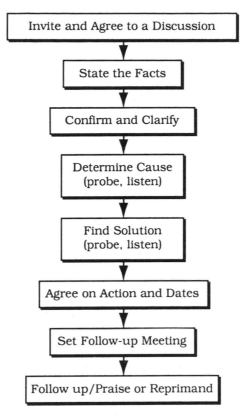

Invite and Agree to a Discussion

State the Facts

Confirm and Clarify

Determine Cause
(probe, listen)

Find Solution
(probe, listen)

Agree on Action and Dates

Set Follow-up Meeting

Follow up/Praise or Reprimand

Goal Setting: Group

You've got to be very careful if you don't know where
you are going, because you may not get there.

YOGI BERRA

W ithout goals, managers and the people around them will
be doomed to operate aimlessly, adding little value to
the organization. Sometimes we set goals unrealistically high
and at other times our goals are too modest. These guidelines
will help you set goals correctly:

- Review the mission of your organization. Identify the key
  elements that can be measured. For example, your mission
  states: "We are committed to exceeding our customers' needs
  by providing high quality products on time. This goal will
  enable us to satisfy our shareholders and provide an environment of security and growth for our staff." The following
  elements would be indicated:
  ✓ Quality
  ✓ Delivery
  ✓ Shareholders' return
  ✓ Staff security and growth
- Call an employee meeting. Explain the importance of setting
  goals.
- Ask for input regarding critical indicators of performance. As
  a guide, choose four to six indicators covering critical areas
  of the mission.
- Establish current performance levels by taking the average of
  the previous few months.
- Set goals. These will be most valuable if they are SMART:
  ✓ Specific
  ✓ Measurable
  ✓ Achievable
  ✓ Realistic
  ✓ Time based

- Set minigoals if goals are large. Smaller goals allow you to celebrate successes more often. Each stepping stone should bring you closer to your final goal.
- Use benchmarking. Compare your goals to those set by other departments or organizations doing similar work.
- Develop action plans that will lead to improved performance. Ask for your people's input. List all the actions together with dates by which they must be completed. Get volunteers to undertake the tasks.
- If your staff doesn't volunteer to help, you can do one of a number of things to involve them:
  - ✓ Find out why there is a reluctance to get involved. Remove any obstacles that your people identify.
  - ✓ Delegate jobs to specific people. Saying "Mark, you would do ____" will get a better response than "Who would like to do ____?"
  - ✓ Get agreement from your associates to spread the workload. Have them undertake tasks on a rotation basis.
- Display goals in a clearly visible place to maintain awareness and focus.
- Review performance regularly. Compare it to goals.
- If performance is improving, praise those responsible.
- If performance is not improving, find out why. Involve your people in adjusting goals to a more realistic level, or better still, find new ways of achieving your existing goals.

Goal Setting: Personal

You've removed most of the roadblocks to success when you've learned the difference between motion and direction.

BILL COPELAND

You will enhance your career and effectiveness by focusing on yearly, monthly, weekly, and even daily goals. Your goals are your road map to a successful future. They will determine the direction in which you are headed and ensure you reach your destination. Here's how to set goals:

- Write down your goals. Don't rely on your memory.
- Determine your goals. Make sure they are SMART:
  - ✓ Specific
  - ✓ Measurable
  - ✓ Achievable
  - ✓ Realistic
  - ✓ Time based
- Break your goals into short-, medium-, and long-range plans. This will allow you to stay focused and in touch with your final goal.
- Make people aware of your goals. Tell a friend, mentor, and even your worst enemy. Contract with someone to meet with you regularly to ensure that you remain on track.
- Visualize achieving your goal. Your vision will give you a sense of excitement and encourage you to keep on trying. At the same time, although your work goals are important, they should not become an obsession. If they do, you will upset the equilibrium between personal life and work, resulting in physical and mental deterioration.
- Act on your goals regularly. True success comes from taking small steps. It is unlikely that you will make immediate

quantum gains without an enormous amount of luck. There-fore, focus on short-term goals that will lead to the longer goal.

- Review your goals regularly. For example, monthly goals should be reviewed daily to keep you focused.
- Celebrate your achievements, no matter how small they may be.

Harassment

The first step in the evolution of ethics is a sense of
solidarity with other human beings.

ALBERT SCHWEITZER

Harassment in the workplace is behavior that attacks, verbally or physically, an employee's sex, race, color, or
creed.

You must act IMMEDIATELY when any harassment issues
come to your attention. Failure to do so might give the impression that you condone the inappropriate behavior. This is what
you must do.

General

- Familiarize yourself with your corporation's policy on harassment. Provide copies of the policy to your associates.
- If no policy exists, campaign for a policy to be established.
- Let people know that harassment will not be tolerated.
- Increase awareness of the problem by having your people
watch educational videos during working hours, or by circulating relevant literature.
- Become a role model of nonsexist, nonracist behavior by
treating your people with respect and always using language
that is gender and race neutral.

If You Become Aware of Harassment in Your Work Area

- Collect the facts. Do so assertively.
- Confine your investigation to those involved and witnesses.

Do not pour fuel onto the fire by discussing the issue with people who are not involved or do not need to know.

- If there are allegations of sexual harassment, determine the severity. Strong action will be appropriate if:
  - ✓ The advances interfere with the complainant's work performance
  - ✓ The harassment has created a hostile or offensive environment
  - ✓ The complainant has been explicitly or implicitly threatened with job loss if sexual favors are withheld
  - ✓ The accused has based a decision to hire on receiving sexual favors
- If the offense is minor, warn the offender immediately in writing.
- For serious offenses, such as offering promotions in return for sexual favors, the accused will probably have to be terminated.
- Seek the advice of legal counsel if you believe serious disciplinary action or termination is likely or if an employee threatens legal action.

Health and Safety

As a manager, you have the legal and moral responsibility to ensure that the workplace is safe and people's health is not in jeopardy. Here are some ideas for keeping the workplace safe:

- Make health and safety a top priority. Let your people know how you feel about the subject and what your mutual obligations are.
- Unsafe practices should be dealt with immediately. Make no exceptions. Allowing them to continue simply sets a dangerous precedent.
- Involve your people in finding ways to improve.
- Find new and better ways of ensuring safety, even if you have the best record around. Keep yourself knowledgeable about current legislation and your role and responsibility.
- Always assume that what can happen will happen. Be proactive. Anticipate possible accidents and prioritize them in terms of probability and severity. Establish guidelines for dealing with accidents.
- Post health and safety rules in a prominent place. Keep information up-to-date.
- Share responsibility for health and safety with your team. Appoint a coordinator who can ensure peers maintain safe practices. This person may serve on a health and safety committee.
- Meet regularly with your people to review statistics and procedures.
- Spread ownership for health and safety issues by getting your workers to present a short topic at each meeting. Your encouragement plus a prize for the best presentation might act as an incentive.
- Beware of fatigue caused by excessive work demands. Fatigue reduces people's concentration and makes them more vulnerable to accidents. People can fall asleep or make mistakes that might otherwise not happen.

- Train people in the proper and safe methods of using machinery and equipment. If hazards are high, training needs to be thorough. Procedures should be documented and properly enforced.
- Keep the environment as safe as possible and maintain good housekeeping practices: Repair damaged flooring, improve inadequate lighting, and replace poorly constructed furniture.
- Review near accidents. They are danger signals.
- Report and record all accidents, no matter how small. These statistics will help you analyze trends, pinpoint problems, and confirm the results of corrective actions.
- Always have on staff an adequate number of people with current first-aid certification.
- Make sure people use appropriate safety protection, but remember that protective gear is a last defense against injury, not a replacement for safety. Always stop work when conditions are hazardous.
- Encourage a team approach. Reward and recognize people for taking care of one another.
- Don't let new employees start work until they are fully briefed on your health and safety rules. Make them sign a statement that they understand the rules and agree to abide by them.

Hiring

Hiring the wrong person is an expensive mistake no manager can afford to make. Here are some steps you can take to narrow the possibility of error:

- Be clear about the kind of person you want for the job. Having the wrong person can lead to:
  - ✓ Poor morale in work area
  - ✓ Mistakes
  - ✓ Extra training time and expense
  - ✓ Extra coaching
  - ✓ Disciplinary action
  - ✓ Possible firing
  - ✓ Time and cost of rehiring
- Before you seek a candidate, analyze the job:
  - ✓ What are the duties?
  - ✓ What qualifications are needed?
  - ✓ Who will the person interact with, in and beyond the work area?
  - ✓ What machinery and equipment will they use?
  - ✓ What physical challenges exist, if any?
  - ✓ Are there any emotional challenges?
  - ✓ How much autonomy does the job require?
  - ✓ Who is the internal or external client for that job?
  - ✓ How does one measure competence in the job?
  - ✓ Are there existing standards for quality and quantity?
  - ✓ Who will new people report to?
  - ✓ Are there any travel requirements?
  - ✓ What is the potential for promotion?
- Identify sources of appropriate candidates. You may look to recruit:
  - ✓ In-house
  - ✓ Through an agency
  - ✓ By advertising in newspapers or trade journals
  - ✓ From teaching institutions
  - ✓ From recommendations

✓ From your competitors
- Consider looking at nontraditional sources of candidates:
  ✓ Retired people. These people have years of technical and managerial knowledge, which can reduce the costs of training.
  ✓ Retrenched people. These are people who were laid off or part of an organizational restructuring.
  ✓ Students. Many universities and colleges offer co-op programs that provide inexpensive help. These people can become permanent employees later.
  ✓ Consultants. Many retrenched people offer their skills on a part-time basis as they develop their customer base.
- Screen resumés carefully. Be cautious about people who:
  ✓ Describe themselves in superlative terms without any supporting evidence
  ✓ Submit professionally prepared resumés
  ✓ Do not show an interest in profit-mindedness
  ✓ Change jobs often
  ✓ Change careers regularly
  ✓ Offer only generalities
- Narrow down the applicants by scoring them for criteria important to the job.
- Contact no more than ten people for preliminary interviews, two or three of whom will be short-listed.
- Send a courteous note to people you do not interview, thanking them for their response and interest in the position.
- Pass on interesting resumés to others in the organization who might benefit from a candidate whose qualifications are excellent but not ideally suited to your job.

Hiring Interview

Conducting an effective interview will allow you to match your needs with the right person. Picking the best person will ensure that the job is done effectively. Choosing the wrong candidate can lead to:
- ✓ Poor morale
- ✓ Excessive performance management
- ✓ Costly training
- ✓ Severance and rehiring

Successful interviews are well structured. In addition to good preparation, they should include:
- ✓ An opening
- ✓ Information gathering
- ✓ Information giving
- ✓ A closing

Preparation

- Refamiliarize yourself with the job, environment, and skills you are looking for.
- Review the candidate's resumé. Identify key issues that need clarification or confirmation.
- Arrange the furnishings in your office or meeting room to promote open discussion. Have both the candidate and yourself sit in comfortable chairs. Sit next to or facing the candidate; sitting behind a desk will distance you from the candidate.
- Bring writing materials so you can make notes on important issues. Don't rely on your memory, particularly if you have a number of interviews back-to-back.
- Consider interviewing with a colleague who can add insight and objectivity to the process. A second person can also help write notes while you ask the questions, or vice versa; after all, it's difficult to make extensive notes while you are listening.

- Schedule enough time between appointments to evaluate each interviewee and document your thoughts. If you do not do this, it will be difficult to make an accurate assessment of each candidate. Preliminary interviews can last up to one hour; final interviews, two hours.

Opening

- Welcome interviewees with a smile and a handshake. Introduce yourself and any other co-interviewers.
- Start the interview by describing the agenda and how much time you expect the meeting will run. Your opening comment might be, "First I'd like to learn more about you, then we'll discuss the position, and I'll tell you more about the company. Finally, I will try and answer any questions you may have. This should take us about an hour." Letting candidates know how much time you have allotted will reassure them that they will have the opportunity to give their information and time to ask key questions.
- Avoid making a judgment too early in the interview. Premature judging will show your inability to listen and to be objective.

Information Gathering

- Begin by finding out as much as possible about the candidate. As part of the process you can refer to the resumé.
- Ask open-ended questions rather than closed questions. Answers to open-ended questions give you insight into the person's ability to problem solve and communicate clearly and concisely. (See page 91, "Generic Questions You Can Ask.")
- Pay attention to what interviewees say. Equally important, watch their nonverbal cues. Look for awkward gestures, loss of eye contact, or change in voice pitch. Crossing arms or legs may mean resistance. Leaning forward or nodding might mean enthusiasm. (See page 42, "Reading Body Language.")
- Avoid generic questions that can produce canned responses.

Rather, get details about specific situations the interviewee encountered. For example, say, "Give me a specific example of how you reprimanded someone," rather than ask "How would you discipline an employee?" Then follow up with open-ended questions such as "Why did you reprimand the person?" "What was the result?" and "What did you learn from the experience?"

- Ask probing questions, relating to the application form, about:
  ✓ Gaps in employment
  ✓ Accomplishments
  ✓ References
- Sort fact from fiction. Most people today have professionally prepared resumés, so it is important to ask people to be very specific about their special achievements, particularly if they look too good to be true.
- Ask questions in a logical sequence. Doing so will enable you to get into some depth on specific issues. Jumping from one subject to another will create a sense of confusion and result in aimless discussions.
- Avoid leading questions. These don't test candidates' knowledge because you give them the answer you are looking for. Ask "How would you reprimand an employee?" not "Don't you agree it is wrong to reprimand employees in front of their peers?"
- Give candidates time to think. Remain neutral. Silence can be an effective way to encourage further comment. Don't elaborate on questions to assist them. For example, if the candidate says, "I missed work once or twice a month," you might get more information by repeating "Once or twice?" in a neutral voice.
- Describe some of the challenging situations candidates might encounter on the job. Ask for ideas about how they would deal with these situations. Better still, ask how they have dealt with similar circumstances.
- Ensure that candidates deal with critical issues. If they go off on a tangent, steer them back by asking questions. Make frequent use of the words *what* and *how*. Avoid the word *why* since it tends to provoke a superficial or defensive response.

- Encourage candidates to explain generalizations or clichés. Ask them to define what they mean in specific terms.
- Be mindful of possible human rights violations. Avoid any questions about people's:
  - ✓ Race
  - ✓ Religion
  - ✓ Age
  - ✓ Marital status
  - ✓ Country of birth
  - ✓ Family planning intentions
  - ✓ Criminal history
  - ✓ Financial position (for example, if they have ever declared bankruptcy)
- Beware if you observe:
  - ✓ Inappropriate attire
  - ✓ Jumpiness or other anxiety symptoms
  - ✓ Avoidance of eye contact
  - ✓ Inability to explain gaps in dates listed on the resumé
  - ✓ Inappropriate comments about past employers

Information Giving

- After gathering the relevant information from the candidate, you should discuss the job. Describe the tasks and criteria for success so the candidate can decide whether or not the job is suitable.
- Describe the company, its culture, and your expectations regarding the position. Don't spend too much time selling the company, so that you leave time for questions.

Closing

- When all questions have been dealt with let the candidate know what the next steps are, including the possibility of second interviews and deadlines for decision making.
- Be honest with candidates. If you don't see a fit, tell them, and why. Don't string them along with hopes that will never materialize. Be diplomatic. Avoid damaging the person's self-

esteem. You might say, "Your credentials and work experience are really good, but this job needs _____, which you do not have. But we would like to keep you on file in case another, more suitable position becomes available." (In a unionized environment, a person with seniority and skills may get the job regardless of suitability for the job.)

Immediately after the Interview

- Evaluate the candidate. A standard form will allow you to accumulate consistent information on each candidate. This form should indicate positive and negative factors, including:
  ✓ Background and education
  ✓ Skills, attributes, and presence
  ✓ Appearance
  ✓ Personality
  ✓ Voice
  ✓ Job suitability

Checking References

- Conduct a thorough reference check of your short-listed candidates. Discard personal friends and relatives, who will offer biased opinions. Focus on the candidate's former boss, peers, subordinates, and customers (internal or external).
- If candidates have professional qualifications, ask for transcripts. If these are not available, check their credentials with the institutions that awarded their degrees, diplomas, or designations.
- Confirm information from candidates' resumés and interviews regarding:
  ✓ Dates of employment
  ✓ Positions held
  ✓ Accuracy of special claims and achievements
  ✓ Competence
  ✓ Circumstances under which they left
- Ask open-ended questions:
  ✓ What are the candidate's strengths?

✓ What are the candidate's weaknesses?
✓ What was the person's most important contribution to your organization?
✓ What will you miss most about (name)?
✓ How do you feel about (name)'s decision to leave?
✓ Can you describe (name)'s relationship with boss/peers/ subordinates?

- Ask follow-up questions where appropriate. For example, "Can you explain that?" or "Can you tell me more?" or "Could you give me an example?"
- Confirm any hunches you developed in your interview.
- Finally, ask if there are any questions that the referee thinks you should have asked.

GENERIC QUESTIONS YOU CAN ASK

- If you got the job, what action would you take in the first month?
- How would you deal with a 10 percent budget reduction?
- What do you like least about your existing job? Why?
- What do you like most about your existing job? Why?
- Who was the best boss you had? Why?
- Who was your worst boss? Why?
- In what way do you and your boss think alike? In what way do you differ?
- What is the most difficult thing about your existing job? Why?
- What are your career goals? How do you plan to get there?
- What is your major achievement of your last job? Tell me how you made that achievement.
- How do you react when you get negative feedback?
- Give an example of how you disciplined an employee. What was the result?
- What was the lowest point of your job? What happened? How did you deal with it?
- If you have one major weakness, what is it? What steps are you taking to improve?

- If I asked your last boss to describe you in five words, what would he or she say?
- As I am going to interview other candidates, what would you like me to remember about you in relation to this position?

INTERVIEW CHECKLIST

	Yes	No
• Were you prepared?	❑	❑
• Did you set up the room to promote an open discussion?	❑	❑
• Did you describe the steps you wanted to follow to the interviewee?	❑	❑
• Did you listen most of the time?	❑	❑
• Did you withhold judgment?	❑	❑
• Were you sufficiently probing?	❑	❑
• Was your language and questioning free of any bias?	❑	❑
• Did you pick up and respond to nonverbal cues?	❑	❑
• Did you let the candidate know what to expect after the interview?	❑	❑
• Were you able to gather all the information you need to make a decision (excluding references)?	❑	❑

Learn from any negative answers and improve your next interview.

Influencing People

You make more friends by becoming interested in other people than by trying to interest other people in yourself.

DALE CARNEGIE

Each of us is dependent on others in our organization. Influencing people to gain commitment for new ideas is crucial. Here are some ideas to do this effectively.

- Acknowledge that you are dependent on others. Develop a collaborative attitude.
- Treat people with respect, consideration, and dignity.
- Deal with peers yourself. Avoid appealing to those above you to exert authority over your peers.
- Help people out, especially if they have:
  ✓ Unique skills
  ✓ Specialized knowledge
  ✓ "Exotic" information
  Do them favors. You will then be able to legitimately ask them to return favors when you need them.
- Treat people as equals. Don't abuse power that you have from holding a higher position in the organization. People will retaliate later. Also, pulling rank will prevent the development of the trust and respect needed for genuine cooperation.
- Keep communications upbeat and positive. Focus on the good rather than the bad.
- Treat individuals as special and unique. Find out what their hot buttons are. Focus on the things that motivate them.

Influencing Senior Management

> Strong beliefs win strong men, and then make them stronger.
>
> WALTER BAGEHOT

You can have the best idea in the world, but if you can't sell and implement the idea, it becomes worthless. Here's how to persuade those above you to accept your ideas:

- Prepare thoroughly before you meet. The more important and controversial the idea, the more you need to know.
- Be frank with yourself. Are you passionate? Do you really care about the issue? Can you project enthusiasm? If not, be realistic about the outcome.
- Collect facts and figures. Data speak louder than opinions.
- Anticipate senior management's reaction to your proposal. Prepare effective responses. Rehearse your presentation with an associate, if possible. Have written documentation to support key aspects of your proposal.
- Your presentation should be concise and to the point. You will not have ages to convince people. Managers' time is valuable and their attention spans are short. If you can't convince them in five to seven minutes, you probably will never convince them. If their interest grows and they have more questions, the discussion will go beyond your anticipated time.
- Collect ideas from those you will be selling your ideas to. This will earn you some measure of buy-in before you start.
- Speak the language of the people you are dealing with. Find out what the issues of the day are. For example, if cost saving is the issue, show how your idea will save money. If quality

is the issue, show how your idea can reduce defects or customer returns.

- Never make exaggerated claims that can be proven false or promises that you cannot fulfill.
- Give compliments whenever they are due. Genuine compliments disarm people and open interest in furthering discussions with you.
- Smile often. People are more receptive to ideas presented in friendly conversation than in doom-and-gloom interchanges.
- Greet people warmly. A firm handshake that lingers a second longer than usual gives the impression that you like the other person.
- Show people that you like them by touching them lightly and briefly on a safe and socially acceptable part of the body such as a shoulder.
- Show interest in their reaction. This will indicate your determination to satisfy them.
- If you are unable to get approval at your first meeting, ask for a follow-up session. Find out what obstacles remain before you can get the go-ahead. Collect any additional information that may be required to fully satisfy them.
- Thank people for their time in a memo. Confirm the issues that need to be dealt with prior to approval.
- Don't let outstanding issues drag on. Show your enthusiasm by dealing with such issues quickly.

Leadership

You can buy someone's physical presence but you can't buy loyalty, enthusiasm, or devotion. These you must earn. Successful organizations have leaders who focus on the future rather than cling to the past. Leaders bring out the best in people. They spend time developing people into leaders. Here are the qualities of a leader.

General

- Leaders have a clear vision of what they are working towards. They don't keep their vision a secret—they communicate it.
- Leaders are consistent. They keep their principles and values at all times.
- Leaders can and will do what they expect of others. They are prepared to walk the talk.
- Leaders are not threatened by competence. They enjoy promoting people and are quick to give credit to those who have earned it.
- Leaders enjoy developing their people into leaders, not followers. They train people to take on more challenging tasks and responsibilities. They develop people's confidence.
- Leaders don't betray trust. They can treat confidential information professionally.
- Leaders are concerned about getting things done. They don't get embroiled in political infighting, gossip, and back stabbing. They encourage those around them to do likewise.
- Leaders confront issues as they arise. They don't procrastinate. If something needs fixing, they do it right away, even if

it's uncomfortable. The longer things are left, the more difficult they become.

- Leaders let people know how they are doing. They reward and recognize performance that is above expectations and they help people identify ways of improving poor performance.
- Leaders are flexible. They welcome change. They don't stick to an old position simply because it is more comfortable.
- Leaders are adaptable. They see change as an opportunity rather than a threat.
- Leaders are human. They make mistakes. When they do so, they readily admit it.
- Leaders reflect on and learn from their mistakes. They see errors as a chance to improve their skills.
- Leaders enjoy a challenge. They are prepared to take risks and encourage others to do likewise. If they fail, they treat the exercise as a learning experience.
- Leaders focus on the future, not the past. They anticipate trends and prepare for them. They develop a vision for their team and communicate it to them.
- Leaders are open to new ideas. They demonstrate their receptiveness by supporting change.
- Leaders treat staff as individuals. They give closer attention to those who need it and lots of space to those who deserve it.
- Leaders encourage and reward cooperation within and between teams.

Team Leadership

- Leaders develop guidelines with their team. They constantly enlarge the guidelines as the team becomes willing to accept more responsibility.
- Leaders change their role according to the demands of the team. For example, they become more of a coach or facilitator if that's what's needed.
- Leaders listen to their team members.
- Leaders involve people in finding new ways to achieve agreed-upon goals.
- Leaders create the opportunity for group participation and recognize that only team members can make the choice to participate.

Listening

The older I grow, the more I listen to people who
don't say much.

Why do people have two ears and one mouth? It's probably
because we are meant to listen twice as much as we talk.
Or is it because listening is so much more difficult than talking?
Listening shows you care, that you have empathy and are
prepared to be influenced. It also allows you to understand
where the person you are communicating with is coming from.
So here are the golden rules of listening:

- Give the other person your undivided attention. Don't do
  other work or take calls while you are listening.
- Find a quiet place to listen. Avoid places that are noisy or
  have other distractions.
- Listen to be influenced. Don't allow your mind to be ab-
  sorbed with developing rebuttals.
- Don't interrupt. Let people finish their point. Only if they
  keep repeating the same point should you interrupt and
  indicate that you understand their point.
- Show that you are interested. You do this by nodding or
  periodically saying "yes" or "uh huh."
- Maintain eye contact without staring.
- Show positive body language:
  ✓ Lean forward.
  ✓ Look interested.
  ✓ Face the person who is talking to you.
  ✓ Smile occasionally.
- Ask for clarification if you are not sure you have clearly
  understood a message. Or summarize your understanding
  by saying "So what I hear you saying is ____. Is that right?"

- Ask open-ended questions. Such questions help get at what people feel rather than get responses that you want to hear.
- Watch for nonverbal reactions during the conversation (see page 42, "Reading Body Language"). Most of what people think doesn't come out of their mouths. So observe their facial expressions, posture, gestures, and eye movements to evaluate what they are thinking.
- Keep pace with the speaker. Don't jump to conclusions or fill in the gaps.
- Don't finish people's sentences for them.
- Don't interrupt even though the person might be having difficulty in making a point. Let others finish before you confirm your understanding. Train yourself to slowly count to five before interjecting or saying something.
- Learn to let short, comfortable silences descend on a conversation. Silence encourages the other person to fill the void.

Measuring Team Performance

If you can't measure something, you probably can't improve it. The most effective way of measuring your team's performance is to involve your associates and customers in the process. A system called Performance Indexing has given organizations in every type of industry a boost, since it:

- ✓ Involves the people who will take responsibility for performance improvement
- ✓ Gets the buy-in of the people who provide the product or service
- ✓ Focuses on the customer
- ✓ Measures a variety of indicators simultaneously
- ✓ Focuses on improvement

The process of setting up a team score card requires the following thirteen steps.

Step 1. Define the System

- Research is the first step. Work with your associates to answer the following questions:
  - ✓ Who are our customers, internal and external?
  - ✓ What are their needs?
  - ✓ How are these needs being measured?
  - ✓ How should they be measured?
  - ✓ What products or services (outputs) are we currently supplying?
  - ✓ What resources (inputs) are we using to meet our customers' needs? A description of the primary resources (people, materials, methods, equipment, and capital) should be documented.

Step 2. Document Your Mission

- Your team should document its mission. The mission will

suggest what you should be measuring (see "Mission Statement").

- A simple formula for writing up a mission is to answer these six questions:
  1. Who are we?
  2. What do we do?
  3. How do we provide the product or service?
  4. Who do we serve?
  5. Where are our customers?
  6. Why do we exist?
- Once these questions are answered, put them into one sentence and modify the wording until the message is clear and simple.

Step 3. Identify Key Performance Indicators

- Your work group needs to identify key indices in the most important categories of performance. These categories typically relate to:
  ✓ Quality
  ✓ Cost effectiveness (profitability)
  ✓ Timeliness (service)
  ✓ Health and safety
- Your associates should reach consensus on what these indices are. Their input and agreement will build commitment that focuses on these key issues.
- Where possible, pick indicators that are:
  ✓ Easy to collect
  ✓ Already being collected
  ✓ Accurate

Step 4. Determine Existing Performance Levels

- Average the performance of the previous three months or another period.

- As you gather data, you will see how suitable your index is. If it becomes extremely costly to collect information for an indicator, then its value should be questioned.
- Current performance levels should be entered on the matrix. Enter information on the boxes corresponding to a score of 3. This will provide more room for improvement than for decline on the 0 to 10 scale (see Figure 2).

Figure 2. Index showing existing performance levels.

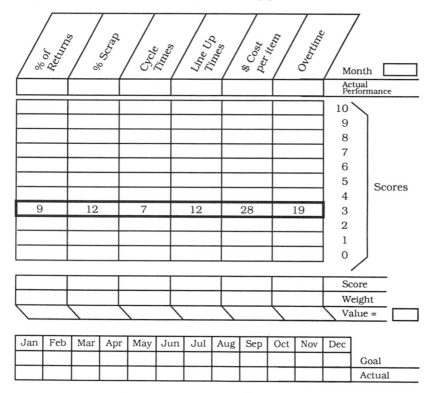

Step 5. Establish Goals

- Next, the team should set goals. The goals should be:
  - ✓ Specific
  - ✓ Realistic
  - ✓ Challenging
  - ✓ Attainable
  - ✓ Measurable

The goals should then be entered in the matrix at the level corresponding to a score of 10 (see Figure 3).

Figure 3. Index showing goals.

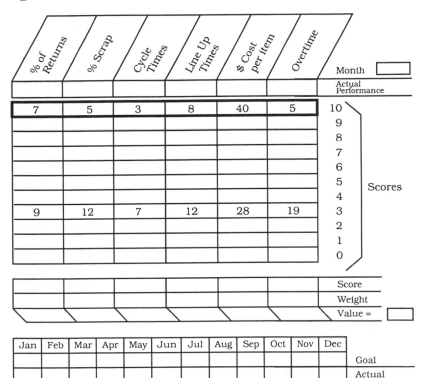

Step 6. Establish Minigoals

- The team will not improve from a score of 3 to 10 overnight. It may take a year. Therefore, it is important that they be able to track their progress towards the final goal by setting minigoals.

  These minigoals are entered in the matrix at the levels corresponding to scores of 4, 5, 6, 7, 8, and 9 (see Figure 4).

Figure 4. Setting minigoals.

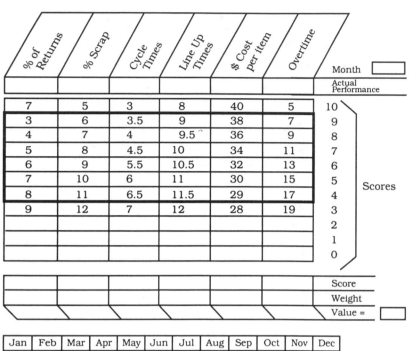

% of Returns	% Scrap	Cycle Times	Line Up Times	$ Cost per item	Overtime	Month	
						Actual Performance	
7	5	3	8	40	5	10	
3	6	3.5	9	38	7	9	
4	7	4	9.5	36	9	8	
5	8	4.5	10	34	11	7	
6	9	5.5	10.5	32	13	6	
7	10	6	11	30	15	5	Scores
8	11	6.5	11.5	29	17	4	
9	12	7	12	28	19	3	
						2	
						1	
						0	

						Score	
						Weight	
						Value =	

Jan	Feb	Mar	Apr	May	Jun	Jul	Aug	Sep	Oct	Nov	Dec		
												Goal	
												Actual	

Step 7. Establish the Lower Performance Levels

- If performance declines, the team should record the declines in the matrix at levels 2, 1, and 0, with 0 being the worst possible level of performance (see Figure 5).

Figure 5. Establishing lower performance levels.

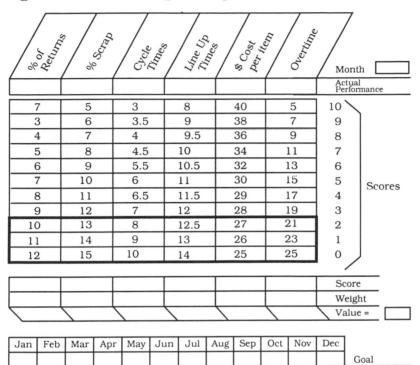

% of Returns	% Scrap	Cycle Times	Line Up Times	$ Cost per item	Overtime	
						Month
						Actual Performance
7	5	3	8	40	5	10
3	6	3.5	9	38	7	9
4	7	4	9.5	36	9	8
5	8	4.5	10	34	11	7
6	9	5.5	10.5	32	13	6
7	10	6	11	30	15	5
8	11	6.5	11.5	29	17	4
9	12	7	12	28	19	3
10	13	8	12.5	27	21	2
11	14	9	13	26	23	1
12	15	10	14	25	25	0

Scores

						Score
						Weight
						Value =

Jan	Feb	Mar	Apr	May	Jun	Jul	Aug	Sep	Oct	Nov	Dec	
												Goal
												Actual

Step 8. Assign Weights

- The team must decide the relative importance of each of the chosen indicators. Their decision should be recorded in the weight section of the matrix. These weights should add up to 100 percent. This weighting, combined with the score, will allow the team to calculate its overall performance level each period (see Figure 6).

Figure 6. Weighting performance scores.

% of Returns	% Scrap	Cycle Times	Line Up Times	$ Cost per item	Overtime	Month ☐
						Actual Performance
7	5	3	8	40	5	10
3	6	3.5	9	38	7	9
4	7	4	9.5	36	9	8
5	8	4.5	10	34	11	7
6	9	5.5	10.5	32	13	6
7	10	6	11	30	15	5 Scores
8	11	6.5	11.5	29	17	4
9	12	7	12	28	19	3
10	13	8	12.5	27	21	2
11	14	9	13	26	23	1
12	15	10	14	25	25	0

						Score
15	20	10	10	30	15	Weight
						Value = ☐

Jan	Feb	Mar	Apr	May	Jun	Jul	Aug	Sep	Oct	Nov	Dec	
												Goal
												Actual

Step 9. Development Period

- The team will need some time—up to three months—to:
  - ✓ Confirm current performance levels
  - ✓ Establish that the indices chosen are easy to collect data on
  - ✓ Devise the simplest way to collect accurate data
  - ✓ Develop an appropriate weighting system
  - ✓ Develop a plan of responsibility for the maintenance of the system and data collection
  - ✓ Plan for improvement

Step 10. Plan for Improvement

- The team should divide itself into miniteams that will be responsible for:

✓ Collecting data on one index
✓ Collecting ideas for improvement
✓ Presenting ideas to the whole team

- Operating units should consider the following guidelines:
  ✓ Focus on problems that members have control over.
  ✓ Avoid working on problems where other people can provide support or knowledge. Ask for their help. Bring them into team meetings.
  ✓ Break problems down into parts. Tackle them one at a time.
  ✓ Prioritize plans. Your team has only limited resources and therefore must do whatever will give them the biggest "bang for the bucks."
  ✓ Work as a team. Involving your team will build commitment and produce better solutions.

Step 11. Tabulate Scores and Calculate the Index at the End of Each Period

- At the conclusion of each weekly or monthly period the team should gather data and plot the results on your chart. The steps to follow are:
  1. Calculate the actual measure for each productivity indicator and enter it onto the performance line of the matrix.
  2. Circle the actual performance of each indicator on the scale. If a minigoal is not achieved, the lower performance level should be circled. Any performance level lower than a score of 0 gets 0 for the period.
  3. Score the corresponding performance (0 to 10) and enter it on the score line of the matrix.
  4. Multiply the weighting factors by the score to get a weighted value. Enter the totals into the value line of the matrix.
  5. Add the weighted values together. The sum should equal the performance index for that monitoring period (see Figure 7).

Figure 7. Calculation of performance index.

% of Returns	% Scrap	Cycle Times	Line Up Times	$ Cost per item	Overtime	Month [ ]
						Actual Performance
7	5	3	8	40	5	10
3	6	3.5	9	38	7	9
4	7	4	9.5	36	9	8
5	8	4.5	10	34	11	7
6	9	5.5	10.5	(32)	13	6
7	10	6	(11)	30	(15)	5 Scores
(8)	11	6.5	11.5	29	17	4
9	(12)	7	12	28	19	3
10	13	(8)	12.5	27	21	2
11	14	9	13	26	23	1
12	15	10	14	25	25	0

4	3	2	5	6	5	Score
15	20	10	10	30	15	Weight
60	60	20	50	180	75	Value = [ ]

Jan	Feb	Mar	Apr	May	Jun	Jul	Aug	Sep	Oct	Nov	Dec	
												Goal
												Actual

Over time, the movement of the index provides you with an excellent record of your change in performance.

Step 12. Plot the Results

- The performance should be plotted on a graph against a target curve that should start at 300 and end at 1,000. A three-month moving average may be used and plotted to accommodate variations (see Figure 8).

Figure 8. Example of an actual and target composite index plotted monthly.

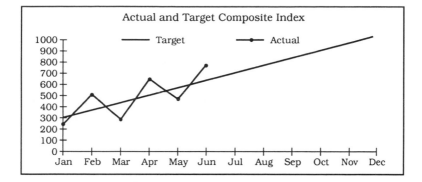

Step 13. Manage for Increased Performance

- Meet regularly to review performance. At these meetings celebrate overall improvement as well as gains of individual indicators. If performance declines:
  ✓ Analyze the causes.
  ✓ Find solutions.
  ✓ Plan for improvement.
  ✓ Take action.

Meetings

Observing yet another huddle at a football game, George Will, columnist and broadcaster, observed, "It (football) combines the two worst things about American life . . . it is violent, punctuated by committee meetings."

There are over 20 million business meetings each day in North America. Most people dread meetings because they are unproductive and don't achieve objectives. Here's what you can do to improve your meetings.

Before the Meeting

- Ask yourself if the meeting is necessary or if there is a better or easier way of achieving your objective.
- Plan your agenda (see "Meetings: Setting an Agenda"). Your meeting plan should state the purpose, items, time, and process.
- Invite key people only. People who don't have an interest in or knowledge of the subject matter will throw you offtrack or slow you down.
- Send the agenda to participants a few days in advance to enable them to prepare.
- Book a meeting room early and make sure it has all the right equipment.

At the Meeting

- Work through the agenda, item by item. Make sure that each item is complete before moving to the next.

- Get organized. Ask someone to keep time, another to keep the minutes, and a third to record key ideas on a flipchart.
- Confirm the objective, time, and process. Get agreement to these items.
- If your group doesn't stick to one topic at a time, make them aware of the problem and give them the responsibility to keep on track.
- Establish ground rules (code of conduct), especially if the meeting content is likely to inflame passions. For example, the group might agree to:
  - ✓ Listen to one another
  - ✓ Respect all ideas
  - ✓ Give everyone a chance to express opinions
  - ✓ Make decisions by consensus
- While you can remind people of their agreement if the ground rules are not being adhered to, you can appoint a sergeant at arms to help you.
- Keep on track. If people begin unrelated discussions, remind them of the objectives. If necessary, offer to put an item on the agenda for the next meeting or deal with it at the end of this meeting, time permitting.
- Pass out supporting materials when the related item is being discussed. If you provide them at the start of the meeting, participants tend to read them and be distracted from the agenda item.
- Keep everyone involved. Ensure that everyone has the opportunity to participate and that no one dominates the discussion.
- Keep the meeting flowing by getting agreements or by asking questions such as:
  - ✓ How does everyone feel about that?
  - ✓ What's next on the agenda?
  - ✓ Are there any other opinions on this?
  - ✓ Can we move to the next item?
  - ✓ Have we all agreed to this?
  - ✓ How much time do we have left?
  - ✓ How will we deal with this issue?
- Before wrapping up, ensure that each decision has an action. Ask for a volunteer to do each item by a specific date. *ASAP*

is not a specific date. It merely indicates that the activity will be done sometime in the future.
- At the end of the meeting, summarize the content so that everyone is clear about what has been covered.

After the Meeting

- Send minutes to each person. Also post them on your bulletin board for others to see.
- Remind people who have committed to doing something of their responsibility by highlighting their action items in their copy of the minutes.

MEETING CHECKLIST

To ensure good meetings, have one person keep a score sheet and provide you with feedback during the last five minutes of the meetings.

	Yes	No
• **Before the meeting did you:**		
Inform the right people of the time and place?	❑	❑
Prepare your flipcharts or overheads?	❑	❑
Check equipment?	❑	❑
• **At the start of the meeting did you:**		
Agree to an objective with the participants?	❑	❑
Agree how the meeting would be run (process)?	❑	❑
Agree on a time limit?	❑	❑
Use others to keep time and do chart writing?	❑	❑
• **During the meeting did you:**		
Ensure the agenda was visible?	❑	❑
Follow the agenda?	❑	❑
Keep on track?	❑	❑
Keep everyone involved?	❑	❑
Get agreements when necessary?	❑	❑
Listen carefully?	❑	❑
Record all key ideas?	❑	❑

- **At the end of the meeting did you:**
  Summarize? ❑ ❑
  Set an action plan? ❑ ❑
Things we want to do better next meeting:
1. _____
2. _____
3. _____

Meetings: Attending Other People's Meetings

By being active, enthusiastic, and focused at meetings you are not chairing, you will help yourself and others.

Before the Meeting

- Find out the purpose of the meeting by reading the agenda. If it is not clear beforehand, suggest strongly that outcomes be established prior to the meeting. If you have not received an agenda before the meeting or at the start, suggest that one be established.
- If time is a problem for you, ask the chairperson if you are needed throughout the meeting. If not, you could arrange to participate during a certain portion of the meeting only.
- If the duration of the meeting is unclear, find out how long it is expected to last. Let the chairperson know how much time you are able to spend at the meeting.

At the Meeting

- Be on time.
- Sit opposite the chairperson. Your eye contact will enable you to respond often and be influential in decisions that are made.
- Participate enthusiastically by offering to keep minutes, record ideas on the flipchart, or help in any other way; you will set an example of commitment.
- Help to keep the meeting as brief as possible. Strategies include:
  ✓ Glancing at your watch if the discussion is dragging on
  ✓ Offering to keep time for each portion of the agenda

✓ Letting the chairperson know if the meeting is falling behind

✓ Summarizing to bring matters to a close

✓ Asking which items are left to deal with

✓ Asking whether your presence is required for remaining issues

✓ Asking whether a decision can now be made on the item under discussion

- If the discussion goes on endlessly, you can help shorten it by asking if someone could summarize. Or ask if the points being discussed have already been mentioned.
- Help the chairperson stay on track by keeping people focused. If discussion wanders, ask politely what the issue has to do with the subject at hand, or if the matter could be dealt with later.
- Avoid starting or participating in side discussions. They distract others from the issues being dealt with and cause a lack of focus.
- Listen closely to the various points of view. Show support for the ideas of others.
- If confusion exists in the meeting, ask clarifying questions. For example, say, "I'm confused. Can someone summarize what we're talking about (or what we've agreed to)?"
- At the end of the meeting ask for a summary, if the chairperson has not done so. A summary will confirm how well your time was spent because it will reflect the extent to which the objective has been achieved.

Meetings: How to Keep Them Short

A meeting should go on only for as long as it takes to reach its objectives. Typically, this takes much longer than it should. Here's how you can shorten your meeting time dramatically.

Before the Meeting

- Ask yourself if the meeting is really necessary. If not, find an alternative, more efficient way of achieving your objective.
- Be clear about the objective. If you are not clear about what you want to achieve, no one else will be and the meeting will drift aimlessly.
- Make sure that the people who need to be present to make decisions can attend. If they can't attend, reschedule the meeting.
- Inform people in advance of the objective and agenda (see "Meetings: Setting an Agenda"). Ask them to come prepared to deal with agenda items.

At the Meeting

- Start your meetings on time. Don't wait for latecomers.
- At the start of your meeting, get agreement to the objectives and time.
- Allocate specific times to each item on the agenda. This will allow you to better manage the time if certain items exceed their expected time allocation.
- Ask for a volunteer to be timekeeper. Ask the timekeeper to let you know if you are falling behind on any particular item on the agenda.

- Avoid going off track. If an unrelated issue is threatening to derail the discussion, offer to deal with it privately later.
- Set aside a "Parking Lot" on your flipchart. Then if issues unrelated to your meeting are brought up, ask if they can be recorded in the Parking Lot and addressed later. Typically, when an idea is recognized, the person bringing it up will let go of it.
- Avoid repetition by recording ideas on a flipchart.
- Run stand-up meetings on the shop floor or in the office to avoid wasting time getting to meeting rooms. Also, people will want to sit after standing for more than 15 minutes, so they will be less likely to drag out discussions.
- Hold your meetings at the end of the day, scheduling them to finish at the official end of business. People will be motivated to finish on time.

Meetings: Managing People

A chieving your meeting objectives will be possible only if you manage the people involved. Since there is a variety of behavior that occurs in the meeting, there are many ways to deal with each.

Dealing with Aggressive Behavior

- Remain calm. Showing anger allows the aggressors to feel that they have successfully caused you to lose your composure.
- If people want to discuss a problem not on the agenda, but which they need to get off their chest, let them vent their feelings for a short while. If their issue is legitimate, albeit off topic, show empathy by agreeing. When they are finished, ask if they are done and, if so, whether you can proceed with the topic at hand.
- Don't allow people to use your meeting for their own political agendas. If their tone of voice is hostile and they begin to hijack your meeting, intervene when they stop for a breath and point out firmly but politely that the matter may be important but this is not the meeting at which it will be addressed.
- If people are totally out of line, making exaggerated claims or suggesting ridiculous ideas, don't debate with them. Canvass their peers to confirm that they alone hold that view. If there is general agreement that the hostile person's argument is invalid, confirm this by saying, "Well, it looks like no one agrees with you, so why don't we agree to discuss this later." Then move on to closure and the next item on the agenda.
- Sometimes a person's aggression in a meeting is symptomatic of another problem. Try to find out the cause of the anger,

dealing with it as quickly as you can. This can be done inside the meeting, if the issue is relevant, or outside, if it is not.
• Take the person aside at a break or at the end of the meeting. Share your observations and frustrations. Ask for help in making the next meeting productive.

Dealing with Quiet and Withdrawn People

• Invite participation by maintaining eye contact and directing questions at them periodically.
• Use the person's name when asking questions so no one else can answer.
• Ask questions the person should be able to answer to encourage self-esteem.
• Sit opposite the quietest person so that your conversation can be directed to that individual.
• Make quiet people feel useful. Give them jobs that will increase their visibility. The role of recorder will ensure that the person is standing up while canvassing ideas from the group.
• Use a round-robin to collect ideas. This technique gives everyone a chance to express an idea. People who don't have an idea can pass.
• Get their opinions on issues by asking questions requiring a yes-or-no response. Praise them without appearing patronizing if they expand on their ideas.
• Give them advance notice of subjects to be dealt with in the meeting so that they can collect their thoughts.
• Canvass their ideas one-on-one outside of the meeting. If necessary express their idea to the group, giving them credit for it.

Dealing with People Who Dominate Meetings

• Many of the same techniques you use to deal with shy people can be used in reverse with someone who has little time for the ideas of others:

✓ Sit next to the person and keep eye contact to a minimum.
✓ Look at everyone but the dominator when posing questions to the group.
✓ Outside of the meeting, point out the problem while expressing your appreciation for the input. Ask for help in keeping everyone involved.
✓ Interject when the person stops to catch a breath. You can say, "Thank you; what other opinions are there?"
✓ Indicate your desire to get a variety of opinions before you ask a question.
✓ Get opinions in sequence (round-robin), reaching the dominant person last.

Dealing with People Who Sidetrack Meetings

• Post the meeting objectives where they can be seen by all. Before the meeting begins, get agreement to stick to the agenda.
• Ask how the issue is related to the subject under discussion.
• Interrupt when the person takes a breath, with a comment such as "Thank you, but it appears as if we are on to something else. Could we agree to get back on topic?"
• Allot a Parking Lot on a flipchart to record issues unrelated to the meeting. Agree to deal with these issues later.

Meetings: Setting An Agenda

An agenda is like a road map that will get you from A to B in the shortest possible time. Having a meeting without a plan is a formula for disaster. Here are some tips on how to develop your next agenda:

- Record meeting goals on paper. Be clear about what you want to achieve.
- Write out the steps or activities necessary to attain your goals.
- Analyze each step to identify whether it involves:
  ✓ Presentation of information
  ✓ Feedback from participants
  ✓ Problem solving
  ✓ Decision making
  ✓ Planning
- Identify a process (method) to achieve results for each activity. Record the method in a separate column (see "Sample Agenda" on next page).
- Estimate how long each item on the agenda will take. This should be a lot easier now that you have a method or process.
- Include as the first item getting agreements on objectives, process, time, and method by which you will make decisions.
- Next allow for a minute or two to get organized. You will want to appoint (or get volunteers for) a timekeeper, secretary, and recorder for the flipchart. While this is typically done at the meeting, it can be done beforehand to save time.
- Record on your agenda the attendees, starting and finishing times, and location.
- Allow time at the end for:
  ✓ Developing action plans for decisions taken
  ✓ Summarizing the meeting
  ✓ Evaluating the meeting
- Circulate your agenda well in advance so that people can plan to attend and prepare their ideas.

SAMPLE AGENDA

Attendees _____

_____

Objectives _____

_____

Date: September 16

Location: Board Room

Starting: 10 A.M.   **Concluding:** 11:15 A.M.

What (Content)	How (Process)	Time
• Agreements on objectives, time, process, and how decisions will be made	Consensus	2
• Get organized	Timekeeper, recorder, secretary	2
• Present report	Overheads or flipcharts	5
• Feedback	Round-robin	10
• Identify solutions	Brainstorming	10
• Pick best solution	Consensus	10
• Plan to implement	Action plan	15
• Outstanding issues	Round-robin	4
• Summary of meeting	Secretary to review minutes	4

Mission Statement

S ome organizations take weeks, months, and even years to develop a mission. Using the method below, you will be able to do it in a couple of hours, over a week's time.

Preliminary Meeting

- Hold a meeting with your staff at which time you:
  - ✓ Inform them of the value of having a mission
  - ✓ Explain what a mission is
  - ✓ Invite them to participate in developing a mission
  - ✓ Show them how it will be done and what it should contain
  - ✓ Show them examples of missions
- Form a subcommittee to do the detail work, if your work area is large. If you have fewer than a dozen people, involve them all.
- Have everyone complete their own mission statement before your design meeting, by answering these questions:
  - ✓ Who are we? State the name of the organization, work area, or team.
  - ✓ What do we do? Briefly state the nature of the product or service you provide.
  - ✓ How do we do it? Describe what you do in terms of categories such as quality, responsiveness, service, cost effectiveness, or any other dimensions that you have control of.
  - ✓ For whom do we do it? Describe your customers.
  - ✓ Where do we do it? Describe the geographical territory you cover.
  - ✓ Why do we do it? Describe the benefits to the internal stakeholders, the shareholders, and staff.

Decision Meeting

- Conduct a meeting to construct the mission. Get the feedback

of each person and evaluate the merits of their statements. Post each on the wall. Underline useful ideas from each.
- Record the mission using the following structure:

Mission of

Who _____
                        (Name)

What _____
                        (The task)

How _____
(Quality, timeliness, cost effectiveness, health, and safety)

For _____
                        (The customer)

Where _____
                        (Geographical area)

Why _____
                 (Benefit for stakeholder)

- Working line by line, take the best ideas from each statement. Write the ideas on a white board, which allows you to change and modify ideas, words, and sentence structure with ease.
- Continue wordsmithing the mission until everyone is satisfied. This should not take more than an hour.

After the Meeting

- Document the mission. Circulate it to people who were not present. Ask for their feedback.
- Hold a final short meeting to add any minor finishing touches to the mission.
- Post the mission in the workplace.
- Have all staff commit to the mission by signing the statement.

- Post the mission in your meeting room to ensure that the mission has a direct bearing on all team activities.
- Identify ways of measuring the extent to which you are or are not meeting your mission. Post graphs of these indicators where everyone can see them and follow the trends.
- Celebrate your area's progress in meeting its mission. When indicators of performance decline are evident, involve your people in finding new ways to improve.

Motivation

There are no people who aren't capable of doing more than they think they can do.

HENRY FORD

Motivation is the skill of getting great performance from your average associate. But you cannot motivate your people: They need to motivate themselves. What you can do is create the climate in which motivation will blossom.

- Expect the most from your people. Your behavior will reflect your confidence. You will not supervise too closely. You will trust them. You will delegate responsibility.
- Treat associates like adults. Adults are respected and listened to. Adults are allowed to make decisions without constant evaluation and criticism. Adults are trusted with important information.
- Treat your associates as you would your customers. Regularly, ask them for feedback on how you are doing. Listen to their comments and take action to improve yourself.
- Recognize people for a job well done. People feel good when they are made to feel special. Their confidence grows. They also become more willing to take on increasingly tough tasks.
- Be clear about your expectations. Be specific.
- Set goals with, not for, people. Involve them in determining SMART goals:
  ✓ Specific
  ✓ Measurable
  ✓ Achievable
  ✓ Realistic
  ✓ Time based

Involvement leads to commitment. Commitment leads to achievement. Achievement allows you to recognize and reward people.

- Give your associates regular feedback (see "Feedback"). Don't wait till the annual performance appraisal.
- Trust your people. Allow them to make decisions without being closely monitored. Also, let them make mistakes and learn from these mistakes by fixing them.
- Don't hover around people. It will make them nervous and undermine their confidence.
- Treat your people as individuals, not as statistics. Show an interest in them. Find out about outside activities, interests, and family. Find something that you have in common with them and use it to establish rapport.
- Meet with associates regularly to review:
  ✓ How you are doing as a coach
  ✓ What help they need to do their job better
  ✓ What changes would make their job better or easier
  ✓ What they like best and what they like least
  ✓ What they do best and what they do worst
  ✓ What their priorities in the job are
- Allow people to make the decisions in their own work area, to increase their confidence and give them a sense of ownership.
- Train people who want more responsibility. They will be able to do a greater variety of tasks and handle more complex duties.
- Keep people informed. Share important information. Take them into your confidence. Make them feel important.
- Identify people's strengths. Find out what special achievements they have made outside of work. Put these skills to work for you.
- Don't allow failure to destroy the self-confidence of your people. Encourage them to try again, pointing out your confidence in them.
- Never betray the confidence of your associates. Keep private matters to yourself.
- Challenge people with an increasing number of tasks and decisions. Allow them time and space to grow. The more they do, the quicker they can absorb some of your less challenging tasks, giving you more time to tackle those that best use your skills.
- Provide people with opportunities to participate fully as a

team member. For example, rotate the role of meeting facilitator.

- Meet daily with them. Let them know your priorities. If you need to change priorities, explain why.
- Respect people's time. Don't ask them to do things that others should be doing, unless it is an emergency. Don't continuously interrupt them unless absolutely necessary. Let them complete each task.
- Introduce your assistant to key associates and customers. All parties will be more comfortable resolving issues in your absence.
- Inform your people where you are, how you can be reached, and when you will be returning. Pressure to track you down during a crisis is an unnecessary burden.
- Don't treat your people as scapegoats when things go wrong, especially if you are the cause of the problem. You will destroy their trust in you and undermine your working relationship.
- Provide people with the encouragement, time, and money needed to upgrade their skills. This investment in their training demonstrates your long-term commitment to them.

Negotiating

The measure of a man is what he does with power.

PITTACUS

Negotiating is the ability to influence people. It is the art of letting someone else have your way. Most people have no idea how easy it is to influence others. People have a lot more power to influence than they believe. There are many ways you can use power to help you achieve your objective. Study and use these approaches to maximize your influence:

- **Precedent.** Show examples of where your idea has worked before. The best precedents come from your own work area or organization. If you can't find examples close to home, look within your industry. When presenting ideas using precedent, say, "I know it will work because it has done so before. Here's an example. . . ."
- **Legitimacy.** Make your idea look legitimate by using documentation. Written reports will enhance a verbal presentation. Information from trade journals, citing examples of success or quoting acknowledged experts, will all improve your case. When you introduce legitimacy you might say, "Here is an example of what I am talking about" or "Here is additional evidence of what I am saying."
- **Persistence.** If water drops on a rock continuously, the water will eventually make a hole in the rock. Similarly, you will wear down your opposition if you are tenacious. You will demonstrate persistence by not taking no for an answer. Keep wearing your opponent down with comments such as "Yes, but . . ." or "When else could we meet?" or "Let's keep trying till we do find a way."
- **Competition.** Let people know that you have choices. They will feel less secure knowing that your needs can be satisfied

elsewhere. So you can say, "If you can't, then I will ask ___,"
or "I can get more from ___."

- **Knowledge.** Let people know about your expertise. Show
  them your qualifications (legitimacy). The more impressed
  they are with your credentials, the easier it is to influence
  them. Also, demonstrate your knowledge with facts and
  examples of where you have been successful before (precedent).
- **Rationality.** Give people the data to back up your opinions.
  Presenting the data in writing (legitimacy) will further increase your power.
- **Rank.** You can use rank positively or negatively. If people
  think that you will make a decision irrespective of their
  opinion, because your rank allows you to, they will find
  ways of subverting the implementation. So if you use rank,
  do so only as a last resort, reminding people only momen-
  tarily of your position.

  You can also increase your power by linking with people who
  have a higher rank. For example, say, "The president told
  me that. . . ."

Negotiating: Win-Win Tactics

Don't ever slam a door; you might want to go back.

DON HEROLD

The outcome of a negotiation can be win-win, win-lose, or lose-lose. Sometimes you strive for a win-lose, such as when you buy a car or a home (hopefully, you win). But at work, with your boss, peers, and subordinates, a win-lose attitude will come back to haunt you. You might win the first round, but sooner or later the loser will get even! So here's how to produce a mutually beneficial result:

- Establish a joint goal at the outset. Even if the parameters are broad, you will focus on the objective instead of beating each other up.
- Establish ground rules for the negotiations, particularly if the negotiation has typically created conflict and emotional outbursts. You might both agree to:
  - ✓ Listen to each other without interruption
  - ✓ Respect each other even though you may disagree on issues
  - ✓ Be flexible on the less important issues
- State your needs clearly.
- Establish what the other person's needs are by listening. If you can meet those needs, chances are the person will meet yours. Focus on what they are telling you instead of on formulating rebuttals.
- Find the common ground first and build on it to solve other problems.
- Prioritize issues; determine what is negotiable and what is not.

- Try to understand what others think and feel. Read their nonverbal language. What is their facial expression telling you? What are their eyes doing when you ask for commitment? And what are their posture and hand gestures telling you?
- Avoid arguing, especially over minor issues. Train yourself to agree to the small things so that you establish a collaborative environment focused on solving the more important items.
- Deal with issues as they arise so that they don't accumulate and overwhelm your discussion.
- Don't get sidetracked. If your negotiations are going off on a tangent, get back on track with a comment such as "Yes, I can relate to that, but could we get back to the central issue?"
- Be creative. There is more than one way to reach your goal. Have alternative ideas that will still provide benefits for all. Rigidity reduces creative problem solving and increases conflict.
- Stop negotiations from time to time to share your feelings. Find out how others are feeling. If they are negative, find ways to overcome the hostility so that you can continue to solve problems in a constructive manner.
- Whenever the discussion becomes vague, clarify your understanding with a summary. For example, say, "Do I understand the problem right? In my mind, it is. . . ."
- In a unionized environment, be aware of items affected by the collective agreement. These should not be negotiated on a one-to-one basis.

Orientation

Having hired the right people, you can promote their successful adjustment to the organization by orienting them properly.

Before Arrival

- Plan to ensure a successful integration of the new person:
    - ✓ Have the workstation set up with supplies in advance.
    - ✓ Have someone greet the new employee on arrival.
    - ✓ Post a letter on the bulletin board welcoming the employee and inviting others to do the same.

The First Day

- Spend some quiet time getting to know your new associates. Learn about their work background, previous jobs, and likes and dislikes.
- Give the associates documentation on salary and benefits.
- Give new employees a tour of the facilities. Show them the key facilities, including parking, washrooms, the cafeteria, and emergency exits.
- Review the company's mission, values, and philosophy if these are available and documented. Discuss how new employees can contribute to the successful achievement of corporate goals.
- Show them each department and how they relate to yours. Also show the major products and services. Information will give people the big picture so they can see how they fit into it.
- While you can do some of the orientation, consider involving someone else. Sending the new associate with a person from another work area can be beneficial in that it:
    - ✓ Suggests that departments work together
    - ✓ Stresses teamwork

✓ Establishes contacts with people in other areas
✓ Improves communications between work areas
✓ Demonstrates your esteem for people outside of your
work area
• To facilitate the associate's integration into the social fabric of
the company, provide a "buddy" who can act as a mentor
when you are not available and provide company during
breaks.

Later

• Do not prejudice the associate about other people or departments by running them down. Allow new employees to form
their own opinions based on their experience.
• Establish an open-door policy so that the associate has easy
access to you when needed.
• Follow up regularly to see how new associates are doing.
Praise their accomplishments. This will increase their confidence and sense of satisfaction at having joined the organization.
• Treat new associates as a resource. They will have a fresh
perspective on different ways of doing things. Be receptive to
their input by showing your interest and, where possible,
acting on their suggestions.
• Schedule a meeting about six weeks after the orientation to
find out:
✓ How the person is doing
✓ What more you can do to help
✓ New ways of improving the orientation process
• Consider inviting a person's family or significant other for
an orientation. This will demonstrate your interest in the
person.

ORIENTATION CHECKLIST

Use this list to ensure your new associate gets off on the right foot.
• Prepare workstation.   ❑
• Explain corporate mission, vision, and values.   ❑
• Review company policies (including health and safety).   ❑

- Review benefit program. ❑
- Give copies of rules, benefits, policies. ❑
- Review union contract (if applicable). ❑
- Introduce to work peers. ❑
- Conduct—or have someone else conduct—tour. ❑
- Introduce to key contacts in other departments. ❑
- Identify emergency exits, washrooms, cafeteria. ❑
- Demonstrate products and services. ❑
- Introduce to buddy. ❑
- Set up training program—technical and soft skills. ❑

Performance Appraisals

An effective appraisal can lead to better performance. Always conduct the appraisal in a problem-solving spirit and focus on the future, not the past. The process should hold no surprises since daily problems should be dealt with immediately.

Preparation

- Update the person's file regularly so that your feedback will be based on facts.
- Set up a meeting time with your associates. Give them enough time to prepare. Don't schedule the meeting for a Friday, especially if a performance problem is going to be discussed.
- Allocate sufficient time. Two hours should allow for a full interchange of ideas.
- Provide associates with a sample questionnaire, which allows them to do some focused thinking about the process and content of the interview, reduces the probability of surprises, and gives them a chance to complete the appropriate form from their perspective.
- Make sure that your documentation is prepared. Review the file so you are familiar with:
  - ✓ Previous performance goals
  - ✓ The collective agreement (if appropriate)
  - ✓ The job description
  - ✓ Special achievements
  - ✓ Problems since the last appraisal
- In your preparation, identify new projects, goals, and standards that should be achieved in the next period. Be prepared to handle unrealistic goals or those that you cannot support.

Conducting the Appraisal

- Set the climate for a productive interchange. Welcome the employee with a smile.

- Sit in a comfortable position next to the employee rather than behind a desk. This will improve communication.
- Set the ground rules for the meeting. These might include being:
  ✓ Open
  ✓ Frank
  ✓ Factual where possible
  ✓ Positive
  ✓ Focused on the future
- Ask the associate for concerns about the process. Respond openly and honestly.
- Next, review the associate's job. You may find that your ideas about the nature of the job responsibilities are different. Priorities may have changed. Or maybe your associate's skill set now allows a new dimension to the job.
- Review the goals that were set previously. Have they been achieved? If not, why not? Were problems within or beyond the associate's control?
- Review the associate's achievements. Refer to your file. Also ask about areas where the associate has been effective. Focus on the narrative parts of the evaluation rather than the numerical ratings.
- Review areas where improvement is needed. Be specific about your concerns. Give examples to illustrate your knowledge and understanding of the issue.
- If your system calls for it, give your overall rating of the employee. If your discussions to this point have been open, frank, and factual, the final rating should be no surprise.
- Plan for improvement. Be positive. Ask for ideas to improve weaknesses. If the associate struggles to identify appropriate solutions, suggest some of your own. Gain commitment.
- Set an action plan to ensure that weaknesses are dealt with.
- Deal with the associate's goals and career aspirations. Be honest. Don't make promises that are hard to keep. Opportunities for advancement are all too few in organizations that are downsizing. Focus on development, personal growth, and providing opportunities to undertake important new projects, should this be appropriate.
- Before wrapping up, ask for feedback about the process. Is

the associate satisfied? Has the meeting met the associate's objectives?
* Finally, summarize the key points of the appraisal and close the meeting on a positive note. Provide a copy of the appraisal to the associate.

Follow Up

* Hold regular formal and informal meetings with your associate to ensure that action plans for improvement are being implemented. Recognize special achievements. If the associate is not living up to commitments, find out why and help the person get back on track (see "Feedback").

PERFORMANCE APPRAISAL CHECKLIST

Learn from each evaluation by identifying specific areas of improvement. Spend two to three minutes immediately after the interview to reflect on your performance.
Circle the number that best reflects where you fall on the scale. The higher the number, the more like the characteristic you are. When you have finished, total the numbers circled in the space provided.

1. I let the associate do most of the talking.   10 9 8 7 6 5 4 3 2 1
2. I listened to the associate's ideas.   10 9 8 7 6 5 4 3 2 1
3. I was prepared to suggest solutions to problems and development needs but let the associate contribute first.   10 9 8 7 6 5 4 3 2 1
4. I did not teach, argue, or defend my authority.   10 9 8 7 6 5 4 3 2 1
5. I recognized positive performance and identified and dealt with problems.   10 9 8 7 6 5 4 3 2 1
6. I supported the associate's ideas rather than forcing my own.   10 9 8 7 6 5 4 3 2 1

7. I invited alternatives rather than assuming there is only one way to approach an issue.   10 9 8 7 6 5 4 3 2 1
8. I used open-ended, reflective, and directive questions to stimulate discussion.   10 9 8 7 6 5 4 3 2 1
9. I was specific and descriptive when I expressed a concern about performance.   10 9 8 7 6 5 4 3 2 1
10. My associate knows I want him or her to succeed.   10 9 8 7 6 5 4 3 2 1

Total

90–100   You are leading successful discussions.

70–89   You have significant strengths. A few improvements are needed.

50–69   You have some strengths but a significant number of improvements are needed.

Below 50 Make a serious effort to improve in several categories, especially areas where you scored 6 or less regardless of your total score.

Presentations

You can have the best idea in the world, but if you can't sell it, your idea will die on the vine. Here is how to get ready for a presentation and how to conduct it with maximum impact.

Preparation

- Learn all you can about your audience. Discover their hot buttons.
- Prepare your presentation. Assemble appropriate supporting documentation. If the presentation is complex have a package of information prepared for each participant (distribute in advance if possible).
- Decide on the best medium for your presentation. The most commonly used media are slides or overheads for a formal presentation, or flipcharts for an informal presentation. People require about 40 percent less time to grasp a concept with visual aids than with verbal instruction alone.
- Remember, your audience will access information in three ways:
  ✓ Visual
  ✓ Auditory
  ✓ Kinesthetic
  Your presentation should include all three for maximum impact.
- Plan your agenda. It should cover:
  ✓ Welcome and introductions

✓ Objectives
✓ The problem
✓ The solution
✓ The benefits
✓ Your action plan
✓ How you arrived at your conclusion
✓ Questions and answers
✓ Request for go-ahead
✓ Wrap up
- Prepare your slides or overheads:
  ✓ Keep them short and to the point.
  ✓ Use one idea per transparency or slide.
  ✓ Add a picture where possible.
  ✓ Make sure that letters are large, bold, and legible.
- Plan your presentation to last no more than 15 to 20 minutes. For simpler proposals, shorter is better. Use the KISS principle (keep it short and simple).
- Assemble all your information and do a dry run out loud. Imagine the audience in front of you. Gauge their reaction. Record your presentation so that you can refine it and adjust timing.
- Assemble an emergency kit of markers, masking tape, name cards, spare bulbs, pencils, and pens.
- Give people plenty of notice of your presentation. Confirm their attendance.

Setup

- Get to the meeting room early. Make sure that the seating arrangement and equipment are as you requested.
- Check the view from several seats to ensure that everyone can see the overhead screen and flipchart.
- Check all equipment. If you are using a slide or overhead projector, make sure that you know how it works and that it does work.
- Have spare bulbs handy. The more important the presentation, the greater the chance that something might go wrong—that's Murphy's Law.
- Prepare places for each person and provide writing paper

and a pen if necessary. However, do not hand out your presentation at this time. People will tend to read your material instead of listening to you. Pass it out at the end of the presentation.

Conducting the Presentation

- Relax and welcome people into the meeting room. Show your confidence and approachability with a firm handshake and a smile.
- When everyone is seated, welcome them officially and let them know what to expect. Remind them of your agenda, the expected outcome, the amount of time you intend to take, and breaks. Tell them you will pass out copies of the presentation after you have finished. Also, let them know where the washrooms and fire exits are.
- Let people know if you intend to take questions as they occur or whether you prefer them at the end of the presentation. The former approach will show greater interest in the attendees and greater confidence in your ability.
- Follow your agenda step-by-step.
- Start off with as much impact as possible. Present a challenge or recall a story that will move your audience.
- Ask rhetorical questions from time to time. Challenge your audience. Conduct periodic polls by asking a question that needs a show of hands for an answer.
- When you conduct a question-and-answer session, focus on those people who are likely to be constructive and positive (see "Meetings: Managing People").
- If a question comes from someone who rambles a lot, you might say, "If you could summarize your ideas in about twenty words, what would they be?" (See "Meetings: Managing People.")
- Paraphrase questions to give yourself time to formulate an answer. You will also give people who didn't hear the question a chance to do so.
- Use questions as a chance to reinforce key principles.
- If you don't have an answer, say so. You can ask if others

have an answer or offer to do some research and get back to them later.

- You can avoid having hostile people destroy your presentation by:
  - ✓ Not being defensive
  - ✓ Not engaging in verbal sparring
  - ✓ Using humor to diffuse tension
  - ✓ Providing facts rather than opinions
  - ✓ Canvassing other opinions to show alternative approaches
  - ✓ Offering to deal with their issues
  - ✓ Offering to deal with their issues outside of the meeting if unrelated to your topic (see "Meetings: Managing People")
- Keep the presentation short and to the point. Don't cover material that is already known to the audience. Focus on new information.
- Do not read word-for-word from your notes, slides, or overheads. The audience can do that, too. Give people a chance to read each visual and then paraphrase the content, stressing key points.
- Provide a bridging comment between overheads and slides so that your presentation is knitted together.
- Maintain eye contact with your audience.
  - ✓ Scan the audience, looking at each person for three to five seconds.
  - ✓ Don't read off the screen or turn your back on people.
- Keep people's attention by:
  - ✓ Changing the pace of presentation from time to time.
  - ✓ Doing something different at least every seven minutes: Ask questions, poll the audience, complete questionnaires, do group work, and so on.
  - ✓ Modulating your voice: Speak loudly and then softly, quickly and then deliberately.
  - ✓ Animating your facial expressions and gestures.
  - ✓ Punching the air on key points.
- Move around the room, getting closer to your audience when they ask questions. Staying behind a podium will build a wall between you and your audience.

PRESENTATION CHECKLIST

Use this list to evaluate your performance and identify things you might do differently next time.

	Yes	No
Did you:		
• Thank participants for coming	❑	❑
• Show and follow an agenda	❑	❑
• Get agreement to time	❑	❑
• Show benefits early	❑	❑
• Use the KISS principle	❑	❑
• Avoid getting into small details	❑	❑
• Show confidence	❑	❑
• Use a variety of visual aids	❑	❑
• Avoid using notes	❑	❑
• Speak deliberately	❑	❑
• Use the floor space	❑	❑
• Have eye contact with the audience	❑	❑
• Give credit to those who helped	❑	❑
• Keep the presentation positive	❑	❑
• Finish on time	❑	❑
• Ask for, not demand, support	❑	❑
• Involve members of your team	❑	❑
• Summarize	❑	❑

Presentations: Using Visual Media

People will remember information that is presented verbally and visually far more than that presented verbally alone. Here is what you can do to enhance your visual presentations.

- If you are using a flipchart:
  - ✓ Write in bold, capital letters.
  - ✓ Use dark colors for words—black or dark blue is best.
  - ✓ Use colors for highlighting, underlining, and bullets.
  - ✓ Emphasize headings by writing them larger, using a different color, or underlining.
  - ✓ Keep one idea per page. Use tape tabs so you can access prewritten pages quickly.
  - ✓ Post key ideas on the walls for easy reference.
  - ✓ Precut masking tape and stick pieces on the legs of the flipchart stand. Use them to post pages onto the walls.
  - ✓ Avoid using markers made from strong chemicals. The writing may bleed through your flipchart paper.
  - ✓ Use diagrams and flowcharts to increase understanding.
  - ✓ Add pictures where possible. Remember, a picture is worth a thousand words!
- If you are using overheads or slides, many of the principles of using flipcharts apply. In addition, check the following:
  - ✓ Check that the light bulb is working. Some machines use two light bulbs in case one fails. Check both.
  - ✓ Learn how to use the overhead beforehand. Different manufacturers have different switching systems.
  - ✓ Focus the machine before you start to avoid the embarrassment of an indistinct picture. Also, make sure the picture is entirely on the screen.
  - ✓ Clean the face plate to remove dirt that will project onto the screen.
  - ✓ Number your transparencies and have them laid out in front of you so you can see the next one before you get to

it. This will help you to bridge the information from one transparency to the next.

✓ Use the four-by-four rule. Try not to exceed four lines per transparency and avoid more than four words per line.

✓ Don't use your fingers to point to items on your transparency. Your hand might shake, making people aware of your nervousness. Use a stir stick or pencil (not a round one, as it will roll).

✓ Show all the information first, before showing each item one by one.

✓ Make sure you don't block the audience's view of visuals.

Problem Solving

Organizations grapple with the same problems year after year, wasting incredible amounts of time and money. The reason for their failure to resolve problems is the lack of a process. Using simple principles, you can resolve problems quickly and effectively.

- Follow a step-by-step approach. Without such an approach, people often start with solutions. Problem solving is most effective when it follows a sequence of steps:
  1. Be clear about what the problem is.
  2. Find the cause.
  3. Identify solutions.
  4. Develop implementation plans.
  5. Track the results.
  6. Confirm that the problem remains fixed.
- Don't jump to conclusions. Groups have a tendency to solve problems before defining them or finding their real causes. They waste time and money since the solution might not remove the real cause.
- Rely on data whenever possible. Facts are always more compelling than opinions. Collect statistics to provide answers to the five Ws and an H:
  - ✓ Who is causing the problem?
  - ✓ What is causing the problem?
  - ✓ When does it happen?
  - ✓ Where does it occur?
  - ✓ Why does it happen?

✓ How does it happen?
- Break the problem down so you can deal with one part at a time.
- Prioritize problems. Deal with key issues first. Alfredo Pareto taught us to differentiate between the critical few and the trivial many (known as the 80/20 rule).
- Focus on problems over which you have control. Problems can be classified into those over which you have:
  ✓ Full control
  ✓ Some control
  ✓ No control
  So clean up your own backyard first. Then go on to problems that require the cooperation of others. Do not get frustrated with problems over which you have no control. Leave them.
- Involve people who are part of the process, especially people who are:
  ✓ Good at detail work and can collect data accurately
  ✓ Creative and can find ingenious new ways of doing things
  ✓ Good at group process and are able to develop team spirit and resolve conflict
- Use a team approach where necessary. Remember, many hands make light work. The greater the involvement and contribution of others, the more the commitment to implementing the solution.
- Don't be bound by old paradigms. There is a lot of conventional wisdom about how things should be done. Sweep it away! Look for new and innovative solutions. Brainstorm (see "Problem Solving: Creativity"). Get lots of ideas—even wacky ones. Build on some, combine others. Then decide on the best. The more unconventional the idea, the more you might be inclined to pilot it. After a successful test, implement it across the board.
- Get a fresh perspective on old problems. Get the opinion of new employees. They probably have new ideas for solving old problems.

PROBLEM SOLVING ROAD MAP

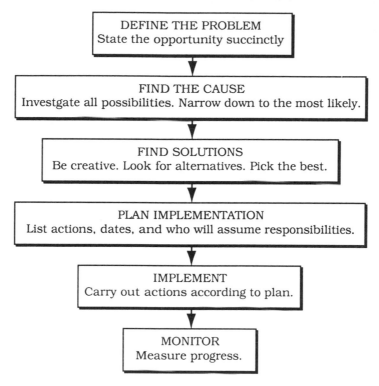

DEFINE THE PROBLEM
State the opportunity succinctly

FIND THE CAUSE
Investgate all possibilities. Narrow down to the most likely.

FIND SOLUTIONS
Be creative. Look for alternatives. Pick the best.

PLAN IMPLEMENTATION
List actions, dates, and who will assume responsibilities.

IMPLEMENT
Carry out actions according to plan.

MONITOR
Measure progress.

Problem Solving: Creativity

Don't be afraid to go out on a limb. That's where the fruit is.

Problem solving requires creativity, but as a result of negative feedback while growing up, by age 40 most adults have lost 98 percent of their creative ability. You can reverse this problem in the following ways:

- Call a meeting of people who have an interest in solving a particular problem.
- Warn people about the meeting at least a week in advance so they have time to do some constructive thinking on the subject.
- Choose a location. The more informal and unusual the environment, the more creativity you can expect.
- Plan to get a variety of ideas by inviting people with different backgrounds and diverse skills. Your customers will add a fresh perspective.
- Include in your group at least one person with the reputation of being a maverick.

At the Meeting

- Before the meeting starts get people into a creative and relaxed frame of mind with an icebreaker.
- Restate the purpose of the meeting. Indicate your desire to encourage new ideas.
- Use brainstorming to generate ideas. Explain the rules of brainstorming:

✓ **Quantity.** Get as many ideas as possible. Don't worry about quality.

✓ **No discussion.** Discussing issues will reduce the number of ideas. Leave discussion and comment until afterwards.

✓ **No criticism.** Don't judge ideas. Early evaluation will stifle the development of unusual ideas.

✓ **Record.** Record ideas on a flipchart where they are visible.

✓ **Piggyback.** Build on ideas. A ridiculous idea might spur a very practical idea from someone else.

✓ **Incubation.** If you run out of ideas, leave your list and return to it later. You will find that participants have more new ideas.

- Appoint a recorder to write all ideas on a flipchart.
- Conduct a round-robin. Ask people to call out their ideas one at a time, in rotation. If they don't have an idea, they can pass.
- Keep the process moving quickly. When you sense that ideas are drying up, encourage ideas from anyone, rather than by rotation.
- When all ideas have dried up, revisit the list so that the team can piggyback, using these ideas to spur new ones.
- Only when all ideas are exhausted should you refine the list. Eliminate duplications. Evaluate ideas based on such criteria as:
  ✓ Payback period
  ✓ Novelty
  ✓ Cost
  ✓ Benefit
- If you are dissatisfied with the ideas on your list, give the group more time to "incubate." Collect more ideas after a break or a few days later.

Problem Solving: The Team Approach

Change starts when someone sees the next step.

WILLIAM DRAYTON

E very organization has a host of problems that have remained unresolved for years. Here are some simple guidelines on how to put old problems to rest:

- Identify the problem through a number of sources such as:
  - ✓ Customer complaints
  - ✓ Observations of poor work practices
  - ✓ Data collection systems
- Form a team.
- Establish ground rules for the team.
- Team members should agree on:
  - ✓ How often they will meet
  - ✓ How they will communicate
  - ✓ How they are to be organized
  - ✓ What tasks are to be done by each person
  - ✓ What the deadlines should be
  - ✓ How committed they are
- Define the problem on paper, being as specific as possible. For example, instead of broadly defining a problem as a "lack of communication," narrow it down to "lack of communication between the first and third shifts." An effective way of defining a problem is to answer these questions:
  - ✓ Who is responsible?
  - ✓ What happens?
  - ✓ When does it happen?
  - ✓ Where does it happen?
  - ✓ How does it happen?

- Investigate the cause. Your team has two options: It can rely on people's opinions or it can rely on data. Data is preferable, particularly when issues are complex and emotional. Opinions are acceptable for less contentious or urgent problems.
- Find solutions. Brainstorm for innovative ways to resolve the problem. At this stage creativity is essential (see "Problem Solving: Creativity"). Consider all the possibilities and then pick solutions that can be implemented quickly and cost effectively.
- Develop an action plan. List all steps to a solution; then get volunteers to implement the ideas by a specific date or time. *ASAP* is too vague and means that the activity probably won't get done!
- Implement the plan. Give the volunteers your go-ahead and then follow up to make sure they understand their mission.
- Complete the problem solving process by:
  ✓ Measuring the outcome
  ✓ Tracking the benefits
  ✓ Recognizing the team
  ✓ Evaluating the process
- Evaluate the process with your team. Identify those things you did well, so that you can repeat them when facing other problems, and correct the things you could have done better.

Process Improvement

S tudies of processes find that activities that add value for customers take place only 5 percent of the time. So the opportunity to reduce cycle and delivery time is enormous. Here is how you can work with your people to improve processes radically.

Step 1. Identify an Opportunity

- Find a process that can be improved. This will not be difficult—they all can be improved! More likely you will need to prioritize your opportunities. As a guide, pick a process that:
  ✓ Is causing customer frustration and complaints
  ✓ Could save significant dollars if improved
  ✓ Relates to the department and corporate mission
  ✓ Is relatively simple to solve

Step 2. Form a Team

- Invite six to ten people to help you improve the process. The team should represent all stages of the process and contain people from two or more departments. Select people who:
  ✓ Understand the process
  ✓ Are concerned about improvement
  ✓ Represent each stage of the process
  ✓ Will make the time to work on the team
  ✓ Have the power to make changes
  If your team consists of frontline people, you will need a

mandate from a senior manager to make changes. Such a mandate will give participants the feeling that their hard work will not be in vain.
- Hold your first team meeting. At the kickoff you should:
  - ✓ Introduce members to one another
  - ✓ Explain the process and steps you will be taking
  - ✓ Train people in the tools of process mapping
  - ✓ Get commitments from each person regarding their participation

Step 3. Map the Process

- Give people a week to collect information about the process from the perspective of their work area.
- At your next meeting, record all the steps of the process on a white board. The board should be predrawn, with the people who are involved listed on the left and the time on the bottom (see page 158, "Process Mapping").
- Note the opinions of participants as you guide them through the steps of the process. Record activities, starting on the left side and moving to the right. Write each activity or decision on a Post-it note. The advantage of Post-its is that they can be moved easily. If you are unsure about any part of the map, leave it blank and continue. You can do detailed research later.
- The process map should show:
  - ✓ Each step
  - ✓ The inputs and outputs of each step
  - ✓ All decisions
  - ✓ The people involved
  - ✓ The time to do each step
- Make a draft of the process and allow team members an opportunity to confirm its accuracy with their peers.

Step 4. Analyze the Process

- At your next meeting, adjust the process based on feedback from team members.

- Analyze the process by asking the team:
  - ✓ Is each step necessary?
  - ✓ Is the flow logical?
  - ✓ Does each step add value?
  - ✓ Are some activities missing?
  - ✓ Are some steps wasteful?
  - ✓ Is there duplication?
- List the problems. Prioritize them based on their impact on the customer, their cost, and their time requirements.
- Taking one problem at a time, find the major cause(s). These typically are people, methods, materials, or machinery (equipment).
- Solve the major cause(s).

Step 5. Redesign the Process

- Based on the team's ideas, redraw the process map to reduce waste, duplication, and time.

Step 6. Implement Change

- Develop action plans for all the improvements.
- Spread the changes among as many people as possible to ensure that the workload is evenly distributed.
- Hold meetings with all those affected to make sure that they:
  - ✓ Understand the changes
  - ✓ Agree to the changes
  - ✓ Will make the changes

Step 7. Monitor and Hold Gains

- Follow up with people to make sure that changes are being implemented.
- Encourage and recognize effort to reduce the difficulties usually associated with change.

Step 8. Measure the Results

- Keep a tally of the improvements. Charting them and displaying them for everyone to see will promote pride in all those responsible. It will also increase enthusiasm for your next process-improvement project.

PROCESS IMPROVEMENT ROAD MAP

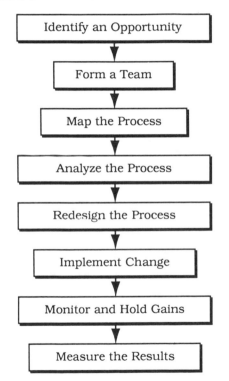

PROCESS MAPPING

Symbols

ACTIVITY

DIRECTION LINE
(for input or output)

DOCUMENT

DECISION

Example of Process Map to
Get a Seat in a Restaurant

Person/ Dept.								
Client	Walk in	Stand in line						
Host/ Hostess		Greet	Qualify Needs	Find table	Is table clean ?	Seat Customer	Give menu	
Bus person					Instruct to clean			
Time (in minutes)	0	3	1/4	1/2	1	1	1	1/2

Productivity

Productivity—the efficiency with which we produce goods or services—is a critical component of being competitive. Here are some ideas to spur you to improvement:

- Determine how you and your associates spend your time. Ask yourself what percentage of the time was spent doing activities directly related to your objectives. Anything less than 95 percent suggests a problem.
- Have clear goals (see "Goal Setting"). Share these with your people. Encourage them to spend time on achieving these goals. Break the goals down into individual goals.
- Measure progress towards goals. Record these and post them so that people can see changes.
- Encourage associates to measure their own productivity so that they will feel responsibility for their own performance.
- Listen to and implement new ideas that enable you and your people to work smarter, not harder. Allow people to try new ideas.
- Give recognition for suggestions. Share new ideas with others in your team so that they can benefit, too.
- Evaluate key processes regularly. Involve your people in documenting all steps on a process map (see page 158, "Process Mapping"). Evaluate the map by asking:
  - ✓ Is each step necessary?
  - ✓ Is there duplication?
  - ✓ Does each step add value?
  - ✓ Where do we experience most delays?
- Focus on doing jobs right the first time. Doing things quickly

will lead to mistakes, which result in poor customer service and lower productivity.

- Find the best way to do a job. Document it. Then train your people to do the job right. Encourage people to follow the most efficient procedure.
- Cross-train people so that they can help one another when work piles up at one workstation. Flexible workers can also fill in for others during breaks, vacations, and sick leave.
- Don't automate for the sake of automation. Make the process as simple and efficient as possible before considering replacing manual tasks with machines.
- Cut out unnecessary meetings. Hold informal meetings in the office or on the shop floor that last no more than five to ten minutes.
- Evaluate the necessity for the paperwork you do. Ask yourself:
  ✓ Does anybody read it?
  ✓ Does anyone care about the information?
  ✓ Does the data prompt decision making?
  If the answer to any of these questions is no, fight to simplify or eliminate the report.
- Organize the work area. Put things where they are clearly visible or can be found easily. Searching for documents often takes up to 30 percent of people's time.
- Review the sequence of activities in your work area. Move people so that the process flows better. Also, move people who work together closer to improve communications and reduce material handling.
- Don't hire more people at peak periods. Get temporary staff. Better still, review procedures to see if you can simplify them and reduce work.
- Benchmark your processes (see "Benchmarking"). Benchmarking will enable you to compare:
  ✓ Measurable indicators of performance
  ✓ Methods and procedures
- You can compare the things you do with:
  ✓ Similar work areas in your organization
  ✓ Similar work areas in other organizations
  ✓ Different work areas in other organizations
- The more willing you are to compare yourself to different

organizations and the more receptive you are to radically new ideas, the more opportunities you will have. For example, comparing line-up times at an electric bill payment office with those at a hotel check-in desk will reveal more opportunities than comparing them with line-up times at another electric bill office.

• Modify new ideas so that they fit your own circumstances.

QUESTIONS THAT POINT TO IMPROVEMENT

Review the following questions with your associates to uncover ideas for improving productivity:

• Is each step in our process necessary?
• Does each step add value for our customers?
• Are some activities missing?
• Do people check their own work or is it left to someone else at completion?
• Is the work flow logical?
• Are related activities positioned next to each other?
• Do we have policies and procedures that prevent improvements?
• Do people have the power to make improvements in their own jobs?
• Do we have data on productivity?
• Do we share productivity data with our operators?
• Have we involved our people in finding ideas for improving productivity?
• Do we have unnecessary levels of improvement?
• Where does the process stop for the longest time? Why?
• Where are the bottlenecks? How can they be removed?

Project Management

Crisis is another name for opportunity.

If something can go wrong, it probably will. Few projects finish on time and on budget. But if you plan properly before you start, recruit committed people, define your goals and parameters, and get a sponsor, your chances for success are good. The outcome will be excellent if you manage the middle and final parts of the project.

Before You Start

- Get a mandate before you start a project. The larger the project, the more important it is that the mandate be documented. It should:
  - ✓ Be clear and unambiguous
  - ✓ Define your parameters
  - ✓ State whether you are to research, recommend, or implement change
- In defining your parameters, you should know:
  - ✓ The geographical limits. Is the project to cover one area of your organization, a single city, a state, or the whole country?
  - ✓ The departments involved. Who will be included and who will be affected? What are their responsibilities in relation to the project?
  - ✓ What authority you have. What can the team and its members do? What spending authority do they have?
  - ✓ Which organizational levels are affected.
  - ✓ Which products or services are included.
  - ✓ Which systems are included.
- Recruit committee members representing the parts of the

organization that might be affected by the project outcome. The members should also be chosen because they have:

✓ The time
✓ Group skills
✓ Subject knowledge
✓ A variety of perspectives

• Plan your project carefully. Know what steps you will take, when they will happen, who will do them, and how they will be done. Get your sponsor to sign off on the plan.

Your First Meeting

• Welcome all attendees to the meeting.
• Explain the goals. Review your parameters. Invite comment and clarification.
• Establish five or six ground rules with input from members. Typical ground rules are:

✓ We all agree to finish our work on time.
✓ We agree to attend meetings on time.
✓ We agree to be frank with one another.
✓ We will respect the ideas of others.
✓ We will let the team leader know well in advance if we are unable to meet commitments.

• Present your plan, showing actions, target dates, and responsibilities. Get agreement to the plan or modify it to everyone's satisfaction. If the project is large and complex, develop the plan with the team to enhance their buy-in to critical milestones and deliverables and to improve the quality of the plan.
• Anticipate roadblocks that will prevent the group from completing its task on time and on budget. Prioritize the obstacles into critical and noncritical items. Get members' input into actions needed to remove potential obstacles. Where appropriate, get volunteers for these actions together with completion dates (*ASAP* is not a completion date).
• Let your team members know what benefits (if any) might accrue to them as a result of the team's success.

Managing the Process

- Monitor the team's progress, especially those people whose activities are key to a successful completion.
- Don't do any of the work yourself. You are the project manager, not the technical expert. If team members are not living up to their commitments, replace them or get them help. The more you get sidetracked into the details, the quicker you will lose sight of the big picture.
- Keep everyone informed of progress. Share success as you go along, to give people a sense of pride and achievement.
- Recognize people who perform even better than expected. Better still, let their bosses know about their contribution.
- Operate within your agreed-upon parameters. If the parameters are too restrictive, renegotiate them before acting outside of them.
- Focus on the goal at all times. If there are a number of goals, make everyone in the team aware of the most important goals.
- Conduct yourself professionally at all times. Your behavior will set the tone for the project. As a role model you should:
  - ✓ Keep out of the politics of other people's departments
  - ✓ Focus on problems and not on criticizing people outside of the team
  - ✓ Run outstanding meetings that start and finish on time, include everyone, and cover a preprinted agenda

Recognition

One of my bosses had a way of saying nice things about his workers that got back to them. True things but nice things. We appreciated it, and we couldn't keep from trying to do more things that he could tell others about. People will work hard to uphold a good reputation.

FRED SMITH, CEO, FEDERAL EXPRESS

Employee attitude surveys reveal that people do not feel appreciated and are seldom told when they do a good job. These same people typically complain that they get instant feedback when they make a mistake. Here's how you can rectify the situation:

- Relate rewards to job performance rather than to factors such as seniority that have little or nothing to do with effort and skill.
- Set goals or standards with your people individually and in teams. These should be specific, measurable, reasonable, yet challenging.
- Recognize people immediately so that there is a clear link between performance and reward.
- Personalize the recognition. Treat each person individually but within similar boundaries. For example, don't reward one person with a pat on the back and another with a day off work for similar achievements.
- Vary how you recognize people so that the process does not become mundane. Some ways to show your appreciation are:
  ✓ A verbal thank you
  ✓ A written commendation
  ✓ Upbeat comments on Post-it notes at a person's workplace
  ✓ A gift

✓ Time off
✓ A free meal
✓ Thanks, verbal or written, from a senior manager
✓ Praise in front of peers
✓ Praise at a management meeting
✓ Praise in the newsletter
✓ A plaque
✓ An award at a banquet

- Periodically acknowledge people in front of their peers: It sends a clear message about the things that are important to you. Public recognition is appropriate for such things as excellent:
  ✓ Team efforts
  ✓ Health and safety records
  ✓ Attendance
- Reward people who have worked excessive overtime at the expense of family lives by sending:
  ✓ A letter of thanks to their family
  ✓ Flowers to their home
  ✓ A voucher for a family dinner
- Don't overdo recognition. Constant compliments to staff will turn the process into a mockery.

Report Writing

Lay down the most complicated movements intelligibly, but in a few words—with simplicity.

NAPOLEON

Communicating in writing is a critical skill as you move up the corporate ladder. Here are some ideas about how to do it effectively:

- Be clear about the goal of your report. Exclude any information that will detract from your objective.
- Know your audience: Imagine what they want to find in the report and anticipate and cover their objections.
- Be a storyteller:
  - ✓ Start by grabbing the reader's attention with a challenge.
  - ✓ Maintain interest with an absorbing middle.
  - ✓ Reward the reader with a memorable ending.
- Use simple language. Don't confuse people or try to impress them with words seldom used. Choose language appropriate for the audience.
- Be brief. Cut out any words that do not make a sentence clearer or more concise.
- Avoid phrases or words that can cause confusion, including:
  - ✓ Slang—"hit the bricks"
  - ✓ Jargon—"this task is really Mickey Mouse"
  - ✓ Clichés—"when hell freezes over"
- Make the report believable:
  - ✓ Avoid generalizations.
  - ✓ Don't exaggerate.
  - ✓ Avoid exclusionary language.
- Address readers as if you're talking to them.
- Maintain an upbeat, positive tone.
- Simplify your sentences. Ask yourself after each sentence

and paragraph, "Is there an easier way of expressing what I have written?"
- Use bullets to list points.
- Use headings and subheadings wherever possible to allow the reader to scan the report and grasp key concepts.
- Keep paragraphs as short as possible. Divide paragraphs that are more than ten lines long.
- Create as much white space as possible to convey a user-friendly style.
- Start a new sentence for each thought. Avoid using *and* or *but*.

REPORT WRITING CHECKLIST

Evaluate your report against these criteria before it is distributed.

	Yes	No
• Is the tone right? (Is it not too antagonistic or condescending?)	❑	❑
• Is the style right? (Is it too formal, informal, or the right mix?)	❑	❑
• Is it organized well? (Does it flow? Is order logical?)	❑	❑
• Is the message clear? (Do you get to the point quickly? Are key issues the focus?)	❑	❑
• Is the report interesting to read? (Is the writing style challenging and interesting?)	❑	❑
• Is the vocabulary simple? (Is the report easy to read? Is it free of jargon?)	❑	❑
• Does sentence structure make it easy to read? (Are sentences short? Have you avoided joining two thoughts using *and* or *but*?)	❑	❑

Amend your report if you have any NO responses.

REPORT WRITING ROAD MAP

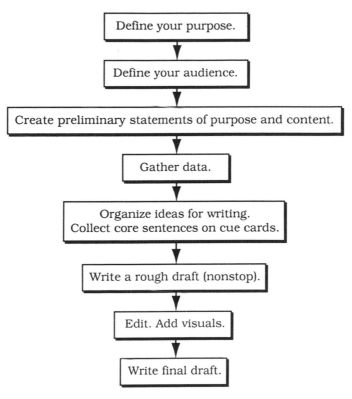

Speeches

One thing a speaker should remember for sure; the mind can absorb only what the seat can endure.

LEADERSHIP

Making a speech is one of the most difficult and intimidating tasks. These ideas will make the process a lot easier.

Preparing for the Speech

- Accept only invitations with adequate lead times. If you don't have time to prepare and rehearse, decline.
- Learn as much as you can about your audience. Find out about their:
  - ✓ Age
  - ✓ Gender
  - ✓ Background
  - ✓ Education
- Establish an objective, something you will say at the end to make the speech memorable. Work backwards to craft your speech.
- Draw a mental map of what you want to get across to your audience. For example, a talk about leadership may have a model such as the one shown below:

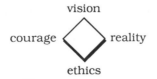

- Develop an outline of key points.
- Order your points so that there is a natural flow of ideas.
- Establish subpoints under each key item.

- Record your information on 3" × 5" cue cards as reminders or prompts. Use one card per key point.
- Don't write your speech out word for word. Reading it will bore your audience and cause you to speak in a monotone, which will increase your discomfort since this is not your usual manner of speaking.
- Practice until you are confident. Your dry run can be done:
  ✓ In front of a mirror
  ✓ Into a tape recorder
  ✓ In front of an evaluator
  ✓ On video
- Avoid body language that projects insincerity, nervousness, or unhappiness. Watch TV programs where interviewees are drilled by experienced investigative reporters to learn how to recognize and avoid negative mannerisms.
- Establish some good closing remarks that will summarize your key thoughts and leave the audience uplifted.
- Visualize yourself making the speech with confidence. Imagining your success will become a self-fulfilling prophecy.
- Remember the three secrets of high-impact presentations:
  1. Be sincere.
  2. Be quick.
  3. Be seated.

Making the Speech

- Dress for the occasion. If you are unsure of the audience, dress up rather than too casually. Dress conservatively for most business situations.
- Grab the attention of your audience:
  ✓ Challenge your audience by starting off with one of the five Ws and an H:
    — Who would like . . . ?
    — What would be the one . . . ?
    — When was the last time you . . . ?
    — Where is the best place you . . . ?
    — Why is it that . . . ?
    — How can you . . . ?
  ✓ Quote a shocking statistic or take a controversial stance.

- ✓ Avoid jokes that could offend. Start with humor, but only if you are good at telling jokes and only if the story is relevant to the subject. The best humor is a story that is self-deprecating. Not only will such a story amuse your audience, but it will develop a link with them since you are signalling to them that you are normal.
- Project positive body language:
  - ✓ Stand erect and tall. Push your chest out. A positive body posture will project confidence and make you feel good.
  - ✓ Avoid putting your hands on one or both hips. Hands on both hips will separate you from the audience since it projects arrogance. A protrusion of one hip signals that you don't want to be there.
  - ✓ Maintain steady eye contact with your audience. Fast-shifting eyes indicate a lack of certainty.
- Use gestures to increase your effectiveness:
  - ✓ Open your arms to the audience, when appropriate, as if to embrace them.
  - ✓ Keep your arms at your sides when you are not using them.
  - ✓ Keep arm gestures between your waist and shoulder.
  - ✓ Avoid quick and jerky gestures since these give the impression of nervousness.
  - ✓ Vary gestures to suit your message. A continuous single gesture will be distracting.
  - ✓ Don't overuse gestures or they will lose their impact.
- Use as much of the space in front of your audience as possible. Avoid standing behind a lectern.
- Create interest by involving your audience and changing your pace. For instance, take a poll or ask for opinions. Find out if anyone can relate to the example you have described. This interaction will show you are interested in, and care for, the opinion of your audience.
- Avoid going over material that is common knowledge. Your information should be news to the audience if you want to hold their attention.
- Use simple language. Words with more than two syllables are more difficult to understand.
- Never use sexist language or say anything that belittles any ethnic or minority group. You will offend your audience.

- Keep your audience's attention and make your speech interesting:
  ✓ Illustrate points with anecdotes and quotes.
  ✓ Use props to add impact. Hold up articles, books, or magazines when you quote from recognized experts.
  ✓ Change your voice modulation. Speak quickly, slowly, loudly, or softly for brief moments.
  ✓ Pause before or after a key thought.
- Tell people what you are going to tell them, tell them, and then tell them what you told them.
- Make sure that your end is as challenging as your introduction. Leave the audience with something to think about.

Avoiding Nervousness

The biggest fear of North Americans, greater even than death and snakes, is talking in front of others. Many a speech has been destroyed by anxiety. Here's what you can do to reduce your stress:

- Prepare thoroughly to improve confidence.
- Use cue cards. This will help you talk normally (with eye contact) and keep in touch with your audience.
- Be yourself. Emulating someone else will make you feel awkward and the audience will react with skepticism.
- Spend a few minutes alone before the presentation to collect your thoughts and focus your energy.
- Before you start, take a few deep breaths to regulate your breathing.
- Maintain eye contact with a friendly face in the audience. Your confidence will increase. Similarly, avoid eye contact with someone who looks unhappy.
- Never admit you are nervous. Doing so will draw attention to the problem instead of your message.
- Don't play with a pointer, pen, change in your pocket, or anything else that may be handy. You will distract the audience. Empty your pockets before your speech.
- If you have a small audience begin your presentation casually with a two-way discussion of something topical. This will reduce tension and allow you to ease into your speech.

- Visualize your audience in a nonthreatening way, such as sitting on a throne or with only their underwear on! They will appear less threatening.

Strategic Planning

Business, more than any other occupation, is a continual dealing with the future: it is a continual calculation, an instinctive exercise in foresight.

HENRY DE LUCE

Strategic planning is an activity usually considered to be the domain of senior managers. But all managers need to think and act strategically so that they can influence the future rather than be impacted by it. The steps you must take to develop a plan are set out below. Customize them to suit your work environment.

Step 1. Plan to Plan

- Strategic planning is a slow, difficult process. Before you begin, ask yourself:
  - ✓ How much time you can devote to the process, including research and documentation
  - ✓ What support you will need from those above, those below, and your peers
  - ✓ To what extent you will be able to involve the people who must help you implement changes
  - ✓ To what extent you want to involve those who can implement change
  - ✓ What steps you will take
  - ✓ When you want to complete the plan
  - ✓ What you will do with the plan when it is complete

Step 2. Develop Your Mission

- Create a mission statement for your department's activities

(see "Mission Statement") with confirmation from your team. Your mission should:
- ✓ Be easily understood
- ✓ Reflect the interests of your internal and external clients
- ✓ Reflect the interests of top management
- ✓ Not be longer than two sentences or a paragraph
- ✓ Realistically reflect what you can do with the resources you have—people, equipment, and budget
- ✓ Be specific enough to lead to goal setting
- ✓ Be general enough so that it will not go out of date
- Circulate the mission to get feedback. Modify it if necessary to reflect a consensus of the opinions of those who will make it happen.
- Post the mission in a permanent place in your department, as a constant reminder to those who must be influenced by it.

Step 3. Evaluate Your Present Position

- Determine how effective you are by:
  - ✓ Looking at your operating statistics to evaluate your costs, quality, responsiveness, morale, and health and safety
  - ✓ Comparing yourself to others around you to develop a sense of how bad or good you are
  - ✓ Conducting interviews one-on-one or in groups to find out:
    — What frustrates people when they deal with you
    — What infuriates them
    — How user-friendly customer services are
    — What policies prevent people from doing their best

Step 4. Develop Indicators to Track Change in Performance

- Working with your people, identify indicators to track your progress (see "Measuring Team Performance"). Encourage your people to pick indicators in the categories of:

✓ Quality/service
✓ Timeliness/responsiveness
✓ Costs/value
✓ Health and safety
✓ Morale

You should not have more than two indicators in each category. Otherwise you'll spend too much time on data collection, leaving you little time for analyzing, planning, and taking corrective action.

- Ensure that your chosen indicators relate specifically to your intentions outlined in your mission.
- The best indicators in each category will be those that are:
  ✓ Easy to collect
  ✓ Accurate
  ✓ Already being collected
  ✓ Measurable
  ✓ Something the team can influence
- If you have picked an indicator that is not being measured, set up a data collection system and get your people to take responsibility for collection.

Step 5. Set Goals

- Set goals together with your associates. Your goals should be SMART:
  ✓ **Specific**
  ✓ **Measurable**
  ✓ **Achievable**
  ✓ **Realistic**
  ✓ **Time based**
- Post the goals and your current level of performance for everyone to see.

Step 6. Develop Plans for Improvement

- Develop specific plans to achieve goals with your people.
- For plans to be achieved in the next 12 months, list all actions,

who will do them, and dates by which they will be done. Also list people who will be impacted by those decisions so that they will be informed.

- Post plans in your work area so that everyone is aware of them. Delete each item as it is dealt with.
- Identify milestones for longer range goals. For example, you might want to establish preventive maintenance programs for 60 percent of your equipment by year 2, 90 percent by year 3, and 100 percent by year 4.

Step 7. Identify Major Threats and Remove Them

- Create a list of obstacles that will prevent you from meeting your goals. Prioritize them. Categorize those that you have control over and those you don't.
- Focus on key roadblocks that you do control. Develop specific actions to deal with them.
- Work with those outside of your work area whose goodwill you will need to remove roadblocks you don't control.

Step 8. Scan Your Environment

- While you are going through Steps 1 to 7, look outside of your work area for trends and changes that will affect you or that you could be taking advantage of.
- Encourage your people to help identify real or potential changes in the environment by:
  ✓ Circulating articles of interest
  ✓ Subscribing to and circulating trade journals
  ✓ Attending conferences
  ✓ Visiting trade shows
  ✓ Visiting competitors
  ✓ Visiting customers

STRATEGIC PLANNING ROAD MAP

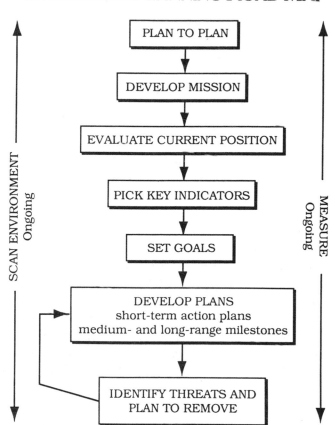

THE TEN GOLDEN RULES OF STRATEGIC PLANNING

- Involve everyone you need to carry out your plan.
- Document your plan.
- Keep the process alive by updating it continuously. Modify your plan as needed.
- Keep your plan visual by posting your mission, indicators, and action plans.
- Work collaboratively with those outside of your work area whose help you will need.
- Remember why you are developing your plan: It is to help you acquire and improve service to your customers.
- Make sure your plan fits in with senior management's goals.
- Keep it simple.
- Don't undertake too much. Taking on too much leads to nonperformance, disillusionment, skepticism, and failure.
- Spread your action plans so that they will be done in an orderly manner.

Stress

The bow too tensely strung is easily broken.

PUBLIUS SYRUS

S tress is a major cause of work absenteeism and a host of social problems. Stress is unique to each person. A few of the most common causes are lack of control over one's work life, moving, and difficulties in a relationship. Here are some things you can do to reduce your stress:

- Accept the fact that stress is a natural part of modern life. Some stress can even be positive since it increases the body's production of adrenaline, which generates energy.
- Identify the things you enjoy doing most and that take your mind off stressful situations. Build more of these activities into your daily routine.
- Break up your working day so that you have time to refresh yourself. Make a point of getting away from your desk to clear your head and recharge your batteries.
- Find a way to exercise. The better you feel about your body, and the better shape your body is in, the better you will feel mentally.
- Establish a relationship with a good listener. When you are close to your boiling point, talk through your frustrations with your confidant. Talking will relieve the pressure. Bottling up your problems can cause mental and physical illness.
- Say the Serenity Prayer to yourself if you are frustrated about something you cannot change:
  God grant me the serenity to accept the things I cannot change, the courage to change the things I can, and the wisdom to know the difference.
- Find an outside interest or hobby. The time spent on this activity will give you a mental break.
- Experiment with your diet. Eliminate foods that contain

caffeine, which can increase your tension. Sugar before bed reduces your ability to sleep.
- Learn to manage your time effectively (see "Time Management"). Continuously fighting the clock is a losing battle. You must change your habits and generate more free time to relax or do the things you want to do.
- Don't use medication, drugs, or alcohol to ease the problem. These substances temporarily mask the problem without solving it. You must remove the causes of your problem.
- Meditate once or twice a day, or as needed, for 10 to 20 minutes. To achieve this relaxed state:
  - ✓ Focus on a pleasant image or word.
  - ✓ Close your eyes and lie or sit in a comfortable position.
  - ✓ Consciously relax all your muscles by focusing on each from your head to your toes, allowing your body to "sink."
  - ✓ Breathe slowly and naturally; imagine a pleasant scene or repeat a key word to yourself.
  - ✓ Don't worry about your technique.
  - ✓ Refocus and put other thoughts out of your mind.
- Learn to say no when others' demands are overloading your time and ability.
- Delegate more of your workload (see "Delegating") so that you will have more time to think and plan. Typical tasks to delegate include:
  - ✓ Routine items
  - ✓ Data collection
  - ✓ Some meetings

IDENTIFYING BURNOUT SYMPTOMS

Waiting until you become incapacitated from stress is extremely harmful. So here's a quick test to check your need to take corrective action (check off your response):

	Yes	No
• Are you becoming preoccupied with your own thoughts when in the company of others, so that you find it hard to follow or engage in meaningful discussions?	❑	❑

- Is it difficult to shake off minor illnesses such as coughs and colds? ❏ ❏
- Are you becoming ill more often than you used to? ❏ ❏
- Are you seeing less of your family and friends than you used to? ❏ ❏
- Are you increasingly short-tempered with people? ❏ ❏
- Do you become more irritable in company than you used to? ❏ ❏
- Are you working longer hours but not accomplishing more? ❏ ❏
- Are you missing deadlines and appointments without realizing it? ❏ ❏
- Do you tire easily? ❏ ❏
- Have you stopped or cut back on your recreational or leisure activities and hobbies? ❏ ❏

More than seven YES responses suggests that you should put into practice the ideas on managing stress.

Teambuilding

Someone said that the membership of a club is made up of four kinds of bones.

There are WISHBONES, who spend their time wishing someone else would do the work.

There are JAWBONES, who do all the talking but little else.

Next come the KNUCKLEBONES, who knock everything that everyone else tried to do.

And finally, there are the BACKBONES, who get under the load and do the work.

Doing some planning before a team is constituted will help you choose members wisely and keep the team running successfully.

Designing a Team

- Develop a mission. Teams need a purpose. They also need to know how they fit into the overall framework and strategy. They need to know why they are being set up and what they must accomplish.
- Clarify roles, boundaries, and expectations. The clearer it is to team members how they will operate, the quicker they will get going and the fewer the conflicts.
- Plan to transfer responsibility. If the team is a permanent one, it should assume as much responsibility for its own management as possible. Develop a milestone chart to promote the orderly transfer of tasks to the team. Ensure a training plan is in place to make this happen.
- Determine the best structure. Decide whether the team should be cross-functional or a collection of people doing

similar tasks. This decision will be influenced by whether your organization needs to break down interdepartmental barriers or create commitment to a common goal.

- Understand the purpose of the team. Be clear about:
  - ✓ What the team will be doing
  - ✓ Whether it will be temporary or permanent
  - ✓ Who your customers are
  - ✓ How you will measure success
  - ✓ What the pressures will be
  - ✓ What those you report to expect

Selecting Team Members

- Develop a profile sheet for each person and position on the team. Your description should include:
  - ✓ Previous experience on a team
  - ✓ Previous work experience
  - ✓ Technical skills required
  - ✓ Communication skills
  - ✓ Willingness to take responsibility
  - ✓ Self-confidence
  - ✓ Appropriate education
- Select the team leader. If possible involve team members in the selection. An effective leader will be someone who:
  - ✓ Encourages participation
  - ✓ Can listen
  - ✓ Understands the corporate culture
  - ✓ Is prepared to take risks
  - ✓ Is able to give constructive feedback
  - ✓ Understands team dynamics
  - ✓ Enjoys promoting people
  - ✓ Can maintain momentum
- Select team members. While ten to twelve might be an ideal number, teams as small as five or as large as fifteen can work well, too. Select people with the necessary technical skills. Also look for people with the social and team skills to complement one another's personalities. Remember, diversity adds strength to a team.

Starting

- Call a meeting. Explain the purpose of the team.
- Decide on your strategy. If you don't have one, ask for input. If you have one, ask for feedback.
- Spell out the benefits of participating on the team. If members see what's in it for them, they will be enthused about other benefits.
- Indicate what the goals are and how these will be measured.
- Establish the rewards for goal achievement.
- Negotiate the ground rules. Using a flipchart, identify key behaviors that will enable team members to work together in harmony. Confirm agreement to the rules. Post the ground rules in a prominent place to ensure that they are not forgotten.
- Identify skills of team members to see how they complement each other.
- Meet regularly, formally or informally, to ensure that momentum does not stop.
- Celebrate successes, particularly those that are measurable. Celebrations increase cohesiveness and develop a sense of pride.
- Allow the team members to take on as much responsibility as they are willing to and are trained for. Increasing delegation of responsibility over time will increase ownership for performance among team members.
- Recruit people with complementary technical and social skills. There is strength in diversity. For example, a natural "devil's advocate" will challenge the group to search for more alternatives before making decisions, which will enhance creativity and the quality of decisions.

Teamwork

I'm just a plowhand from Arkansas, but I have learned how to hold a team together . . . how to lift some men up, how to calm down others, until they've got one heartbeat together. . . .

BEAR BRYANT, LEGENDARY FOOTBALL COACH

M aintaining performance at a high level for the benefit of your customers is essential. You can sustain and even improve performance if you do the following:

- Measure critical indicators of your success such as:
  ✓ Quality
  ✓ Timeliness
  ✓ Cost effectiveness
- Display these measures prominently so that people can track the impact of their efforts immediately.
- Set team—rather than individual—goals for key indicators.
- Provide regular feedback on team performance to members. Your feedback will build involvement, commitment, and a sense of pride as results improve.
- Celebrate improvements to promote a sense of pride and team cohesiveness. Celebrating can be as simple as a "thank you" at a spontaneous meeting on the shop floor or a luncheon off-site. Some teams develop their own ceremonies and symbols, such as ringing a bell when new records have been established. Encourage unique ways of celebrating, even though they might be out of character with the corporate culture.
- If performance declines, don't look for victims. Involve the team in problem solving. Find out why performance has dropped and ask for ideas on how to improve.
- Develop action plans for improvement. Involve the team in

this process. Develop a list of actions with specific dates for implementation. Ask team members to take responsibility.

- Set aside time for having fun at the beginning of a meeting, at the end of a day, or outside of working hours.
- Encourage the development of a team subculture. The group will develop its own ceremonies and symbols to promote its sense of being unique.
- Have high expectations of the team. Challenge people at all times. Let them know the extent of your confidence in them.
- Encourage job rotation, if your technology allows it. The benefits include:
  ✓ Less monotony
  ✓ Learning new skills
  ✓ Personal growth
  ✓ Empathy for one another's problems
  ✓ Shared ownership of performance
  ✓ Improved productivity
  ✓ Less downtime
- Reward collaborative behavior. Encourage team members to pitch in and help one another when workloads have become difficult for a few members of the team.
- Encourage people to get to know one another on a personal level, without unduly invading people's privacy.
- Involve the team in the decision to recruit new members. Recruit people with well-developed interpersonal skills. Knowing how to listen, give feedback, and manage conflict are critical skills for effective team members.
- Establish ground rules. Allow members to monitor and deal with transgressors.
- Remove poor performers and continuously negative people. They will sap the energy of the team and cause dissension.

SURVEY TO MEASURE TEAM MORALE

This survey will establish what you like about the team and what you dislike. The data will be used to identify ongoing opportunities to enhance each member's satisfaction in the team.

Your best response is always what you really think. Avoiding difficult issues will prevent them from being dealt with openly and honestly.

Read the questions below and circle the response that best reflects how you feel.

1 = strongly disagree; 2 = disagree; 3 = neither agree nor disagree; 4 = agree; 5 = strongly agree.

	Strongly Disagree			**Strongly Agree**	

INVOLVEMENT
People on our team always feel included because we:

1. Share information openly	1	2	3	4	5
2. Make decisions after including all opinions	1	2	3	4	5
3. Do not work in cliques	1	2	3	4	5

COOPERATION
People work well together because we:

1. Pitch in and help one another	1	2	3	4	5
2. Offer to help if someone is under pressure	1	2	3	4	5
3. Try to make sure that workloads are evenly spread	1	2	3	4	5

COMMUNICATION
Communication in the team is effective because we:

1. Express ourselves openly and honestly	1	2	3	4	5
2. Have no hidden agendas	1	2	3	4	5
3. Don't discuss people behind their backs	1	2	3	4	5
4. Give feedback to one another as needed	1	2	3	4	5

ORGANIZATION
Our team is well organized in that:

1. Our roles are clearly defined	1	2	3	4	5
2. Goals are specific	1	2	3	4	5

3. Responsibilities are clear	1	2	3	4	5
4. We use the talents of our people fully	1	2	3	4	5
5. We have productive meetings	1	2	3	4	5
6. Tasks get done on time	1	2	3	4	5
7. Our systems are effective	1	2	3	4	5

IMPROVEMENT

Our team gets better all the time because we:

1. Continuously improve our systems/methods	1	2	3	4	5
2. Try new things	1	2	3	4	5
3. Take risks	1	2	3	4	5
4. Focus on the future, not on the past	1	2	3	4	5
5. Are customer driven	1	2	3	4	5
6. Track our results and improvements	1	2	3	4	5
7. Are able to learn new skills	1	2	3	4	5

ATMOSPHERE

It is great to be on the team because we:

1. Have a lot of fun	1	2	3	4	5
2. Celebrate successes	1	2	3	4	5
3. Treat each other as individuals, not employees	1	2	3	4	5
4. All have the ability to influence decisions	1	2	3	4	5
5. Have ground rules that we adhere to	1	2	3	4	5
6. Trust each other	1	2	3	4	5
7. Can speak our minds without fear	1	2	3	4	5
8. Are treated like adults	1	2	3	4	5

LEADERSHIP

Our leader:

1. Is interested in what we have to say	1	2	3	4	5

2. Consults us before making any   1 2 3 4 5
   changes affecting our work
3. Looks for opportunities to   1 2 3 4 5
   delegate interesting work to us
4. Encourages teamwork   1 2 3 4 5
5. Acts as a coach (devotes enough 1 2 3 4 5
   time training us in key skills)
6. Is concerned about our   1 2 3 4 5
   development
7. Shares important information   1 2 3 4 5
   readily
8. Is a person I respect   1 2 3 4 5

Termination

Firing people is a manager's most difficult task. You may have to terminate people after verbal and written warnings if they fail to improve their performance. Immediate termination is possible if a person:
- ✓ Steals
- ✓ Destroys company property
- ✓ Is grossly insubordinate
- ✓ Falsifies time cards
- ✓ Is absent for an extended period of time
- ✓ Engages in criminal behavior

Here's what you can do to make the process as painless as possible.

Before the Meeting

- Schedule the session carefully. A dismissal on Monday to Wednesday will give the person an opportunity to set up interviews with the unemployment office, relocation counsellor, job search firms, and personal network.
- Avoid terminating someone on the person's birthday or just before Christmas. Your insensitivity will make the trauma worse.
- Determine whether the dismissal will be with or without just cause. *Just cause* means that you have good reason to fire the person. *Without cause* suggests that the reasons for termination might be more frivolous, such as a personality conflict.
- If you have just cause, decide whether you have all the necessary documentation to substantiate the dismissal, including:
  - ✓ Copies of written warnings
  - ✓ Copies of all incidents of unacceptable performance, including dates and circumstances
- Consult legal counsel to determine the appropriate and fair

severance package or notice period. The notice period is influenced by the employee's:

✓ Age
✓ Position
✓ Years of service
✓ Education
✓ Salary

- If the associate is being terminated for economic reasons and is in the middle of a project, try to delay termination until the project is complete. This will not only help you, but it will give the associate a sense of achievement, which will increase confidence when job searching.
- Prepare for the interview. Get your facts and documentation together. You may want to script what you wish to say, particularly if you have little or no experience with this process.
- Include a third party, such as a human resources professional, to act as a witness or provide emotional support. If you have arranged outside placement services, then you should include the counsellor.
- Conduct the meeting in a private office or room away from the eyes of fellow associates.

During the Meeting

- Show respect for the person at all times. The process is invariably devastating.
- Be brief and businesslike; do not engage in frivolous, unrelated discussion to establish rapport.
- At the outset state that the decision to terminate (with or without cause) has been made and, if appropriate, state why. Make it clear that the decision is irreversible and not open to negotiation.
- Present the facts leading up to the decision, emphasizing the nature and implication of the culminating incident.
- If the decision to terminate is economic, emphasize that the decision is not personal and that the organization will do everything reasonable to help the associate find alternative employment.

- Discuss why other alternatives were not chosen.
- Limit the session to about ten minutes.
- Review the details of the severance package, including:
  - ✓ Any benefit continuance
  - ✓ The severance offer
  - ✓ Release
  - ✓ Reference (if appropriate)
  - ✓ Any outplacement services
  - ✓ Record of employment
  - ✓ Final paycheck
- Do not offer a good (inaccurate) reference in return for the person's agreement to your severance package. Your misrepresentation could be a legal liability if a future employer discovers you have distorted the truth.
- Discuss why it is necessary for the person to leave immediately to avoid embarrassing meetings or justifications to colleagues.
- Allow the outplacement counsellor some time with the person to coordinate the associate's leaving the premises. The person may also use this time to vent any frustration.
- Obtain any company property from the associate such as ID cards, keys, phone cards.
- Make arrangements for returning personal effects.
- Escort the person off the premises and if necessary arrange for a taxi. Alternative transportation is recommended because the person may be too upset to drive safely.

Time Management

Time is nature's way of keeping everything from happening at once.

M anaging time effectively will enable you to balance work and personal life. It will reduce stress and improve your health. Above all it will improve your career since you will spend more time satisfying your internal and external customers.

Time is a precious commodity because it is a nonrenewable resource. If used poorly or inappropriately, it cannot be recovered. Furthermore, time wastage causes unnecessary stress, can lead to missed deadlines, and can result in poor client service. Here are some practical ideas that will help you manage your time more effectively.

Getting Started

- Visit your office over a weekend and clean house:
  - ✓ Throw away miscellaneous pieces of paper such as Post-it notes.
  - ✓ Record all your information in one system.
  - ✓ Improve your filing system.
  - ✓ Put things where you can gain access to information quickly and easily.
- Analyze how you spend your time. Use labels: A for time spent serving a customer (internal or external); B for time spent on tasks helping someone who is helping a customer; C for time spent on activities that do not benefit customers directly or indirectly (this includes fun office activities). Record your time spent doing A, B, and C activities over a couple of typical days. Categorize the time. Analyze how

much of your time was wasted and make note of the circumstances under which this occurred.

- Develop a plan to reduce B activities. Write down the plan.
  Commit to implementation. Consult the plan often.
- Plan the occasional C activity. Having fun and doing the
  things you enjoy should be done to preserve your sanity! But
  don't get too caught up in those activities lest they interfere
  with the A items.
- Invest in a time management system—manual or computer-
  ized—to give you a structure to work with.

Daily

- Start each day with a list of all the activities you wish
  to accomplish.
- Next, categorize and prioritize each activity as "1" or "2"
  activities. Activities classified as 1s are those that if not done
  will either adversely affect your reputation or negatively
  impact your customer service. Any others are 2s.
- Plan to do all 1 activities first. However, avoid committing
  more than 70 percent of your day to 1 activities since unfore-
  seen problems will invariably upset your plans and use up
  unavailable time.
- Allocate 2 items to other dates in your calendar, not necessar-
  ily the next day.
- Keep your daily checklist handy at all times. The list will
  have little value if you are constantly searching for it.
- Keep your desk clean. Put things where you can find them.
- Use your travel time effectively. Most planes and trains now
  have phones, and you can use your laptop computer with
  little interruption.
- Your car can be turned into an education center where you
  listen to management audiocassettes. Challenge yourself to
  write down the highlights of a cassette while you are enjoy-
  ing your first morning coffee.
- Avoid meetings that are noncritical. If your sole purpose for
  going to a meeting is to get information, you can get it from
  the minutes.
- Delegate your routine work to associates so that you can

tackle planning, problems, and challenging tasks (see "Delegating").

- Do only one thing at a time, and complete it before taking on the next task.
- Get those you work with to respect your quiet time, time when you are planning the day's activities (first hour) or cleaning your desk at the end of the day.
- Avoid procrastination. Identify and deal with the source of your discomfort. The longer you procrastinate, the higher your stress level.
- Do less pleasant but important items first. You will gain a sense of relief and achievement.

Time Management: Avoiding Time Wasters

Procrastination is the thief of time.

No one is perfect. Everyone wastes some time. The three activities that waste the most time are long meetings, interruptions, and telephone calls. Here is how you can reduce each dramatically.

Meetings

- Avoid setting or attending unnecessary meetings.
- Prepare a detailed agenda (see "Meetings: Setting an Agenda").
- Get someone to monitor time and to inform participants if they are falling behind schedule.
- At the start of the meeting obtain agreement on the objective(s) to keep a focus and avoid time-consuming discussions on unrelated topics.
- Record ideas on a flipchart to reduce repetition.
- Avoid dealing with items not on the agenda. If someone goes off on a tangent:
  - ✓ Politely ask what the matter has to do with the agreed-upon objective.
  - ✓ Ask if the item can be dealt with later or outside the meeting.
  - ✓ Put the item in the Parking Lot (recorded on a separate flipchart) to be dealt with at an agreed-upon time.

Office Interruptions

- Stand when people come in to chat. This will prevent them from getting comfortable.
- Ask them if it's important.
- Ask them if you can talk later in their office, a place where you can control the length of the conversation.
- Walk out long enough to get them out of your office and then sneak back to continue your work.
- Close your door.

Telephone

- Leave complete messages for people who are not available so they won't have to call back.
- Install a voice-mail system.
- Return calls to people's voice mail after business hours.
- Train your associates to deal with routine issues on your behalf and to screen your calls when you are under pressure.
- Avoid unnecessary chitchat by answering with your name followed by a question such as "How may I help you?"
- Increase your chances of speaking to someone after you are told that the person is "away from her desk" or "in a meeting" by asking:
  - ✓ "Could you find her for me?"
  - ✓ "Can he be interrupted?"
  - ✓ "I'm returning her call, which was important."

Paperwork

- Keep your desk clean. Put things where you can find them. Don't put documents in temporary places.
- Deal with each piece of paper once. File it, respond to it, or dump it.
- Reduce time by responding to correspondence in writing on the letter. Fax it back, or photocopy it and send it back.

Training

Training is a lot cheaper than ignorance. On-the-job training in technical, interpersonal, team, and business skills is a key component of any manager's duties. Here are some ideas to help:

- Establish career and organization goals for each person in your area. This information will give you an idea of how much time you need to devote to the development of each person. Those with the highest ambitions and those with the lowest level of skills will require the most training.
- Determine what kind of training to give. There are many ways of training people:
  - ✓ Job rotation will give your associate a wider perspective and additional job skills.
  - ✓ Cross training enables people to substitute for one another during temporary absences.
  - ✓ Task forces and other temporary problem-solving groups focus on customer service, process improvement, and product/service development.
  - ✓ Delegation of additional responsibilities enables people to learn more challenging tasks and increase their opportunities to demonstrate managerial talent.
  - ✓ Ensure that associates get feedback on their progress. This feedback can be from you, from a peer, or through self-evaluation.
- When training people yourself, walk the associate through four steps:
  1. Explain the task, why it needs to be done, and how it should be done.
  2. Demonstrate the task. If the task is long and complex, break it down into bite-size pieces (modules) and sequences, doing one part at a time.
  3. Ask trainees to try the task while you observe them. Note things that they do well as well as mistakes.

    4. Give the trainees feedback. Praise any progress to increase their confidence. Be specific about what they did well.

- In the event that you notice a mistake, review your instructions through description and demonstration. Ask trainees to confirm their understanding of the task before trying it again.
- If you have demonstrated a task more than three times and the trainee is unable to learn the task, consider breaking the task down even further. If this cannot be done, or has already been done, it is likely that your trainee is not suited for the job.
- Establish the trainee's preferred method of learning. Some people learn best by hearing, others by seeing, and others by doing. If it is difficult to decide which is the trainee's preferred method, or you are training more than one person, use all three instruction methods.

Unions

Organizations that do not meet the needs of their people are prone to unionization. In unionized companies people feel powerless and perceive unions as better able to help employees. But a union can reduce your flexibility with staff and interfere with your ability to communicate effectively. Here's how you can create an environment in which your people will have little interest in being unionized:

- Stay in touch with your people informally. Walk around. Ask people how things are going for them. Don't respond only to what they say, but to their body language. Probe if you feel there is a problem.
- Establish a formal process to identify and eliminate problems. For example, have a breakfast meeting with a cross section of employees each month or conduct an annual attitude survey to measure the magnitude of concerns, so that they can be tracked (see "Attitude Survey").
- Survey attitudes regularly. Break the data down by subject and control. Prioritize and deal with the items you control.
- Refer to your people in appreciative terms. *Partners* and *associates* are more endearing terms than *employees* and *subordinates.*
- Continuously find new ways to improve working conditions. Encourage your associates to develop action plans for things they have control of. Take care of other items under your control.

- Treat your people as equals. Share information with them about:
  - ✓ Finances
  - ✓ Sales figures
  - ✓ New products
  - ✓ Production forecasts
  - ✓ Future staffing expectations
- Balance the financial goals of your business with the needs of your associates. People will not allow you to take advantage of them for a minute longer than is necessary. Share your research about salaries and benefits in your industry with your people.
- Compensate your people fairly. If business warrants it, pay the same as union organizations. Your flexibility and motivated staff will give you a competitive advantage.
- Make your human resources policies known to all. If your people raise concern about these policies, solve them quickly. If you cannot, ensure that there is a grievance process that is responsive, easy to access, and free of retribution.
- Encourage the involvement and input of employees in human resources program development and review. Treat employees as customers of the organization; design programs with employee interests as well as business in mind.
- Support your staff in cultivating their individual and team problem-solving skills through formal training and coaching, and recognize success in applying these skills. People who are comfortable addressing their problems themselves have less reason to look elsewhere for help in dealing with problems.

Unions: Working With Your Union

U nions are an important part of our labor and employment structure: They protect workers from unfair treatment and even exploitation. While their influence has been in steady decline over the past half century, it is critical for you to manage your relationship with your unionized staff effectively, to prevent costly grievances, work stoppages, and strikes. Here's what you can do:

- Come to terms with the fact that your people are unionized. The chances of decertifying are remote. So learn to manage the relationship for the advantage of all concerned.
- Treat union people as part of the family, not as the enemy. Think of them as customers. People will respond positively to a constructive and open work environment.
- Treat union representatives as your peers and partners so that they will be less inclined to treat you as a foe. Your relationship must be constantly nurtured; trust takes a long time to build.
- Be prepared for ups and downs in the relationship with your union representative. However, if you consider the union a legitimate partner, the ups will be greater than the downs, and you will be able to count on its cooperation in the daily running of your area.
- Understand the differences between the union's objectives and those of your company, but look for commonality and build on it. Make sure that new initiatives can benefit all and that they do not infringe on your collective agreement. If they could, work with your union representatives to resolve the issue with a win-win outcome.
- Review your contract thoroughly. Consult your labor relations expert if you have difficulties with interpretation.
- Respect your contract: It was negotiated in good faith. Learn to live within the spirit and letter of the agreement.

- Be careful about bending rules. Bending rules establishes precedents that the union could seek to perpetuate. Do so only if there is agreement on the part of the union that this will be an exception, not the rule.
- Make sure your leadership style is based on fairness, integrity, and consistency.
- If the grievances in your area are unusually high, evaluate causes and develop solutions to address concerns.
- Meet regularly with your shop steward to share information, formally or informally. Your behavior at these encounters should indicate a sincere willingness to cooperate.
- Keep your shop steward informed of all issues affecting union workers. The more open you are, the easier it will be for you to tap into the grapevine. Often union people are better informed than managers about upcoming changes.
- If your organization wants significant changes in the next contract, work with your union representatives to prepare them and the membership for the new ideas. You can do this by:
  ✓ Sharing your thinking regularly so that new ideas do not come as a surprise later on.
  ✓ Giving people articles describing how other organizations have managed similar changes successfully.
  ✓ Visiting other organizations that have made a dramatic change, to see how it has impacted their people. You can then plan to avoid their mistakes.

Workshops

Give a man a fish and you feed him for a day. Teach a man to fish and he will be fed for the rest of his life.

Chinese Proverb

As a manager, you have skills that can be transferred to others. An effective way to teach others is to run a workshop.

Planning the Session

- Time your training so that it is not too early or too late. If you time your session too far in advance of when people need to use the skills, they will forget them. Training after they have started will require some unlearning since they may have developed bad habits.
- Ask yourself whether the training will benefit your customers—internal or external. If not, don't waste your time and the organization's money.
- Determine whether people need knowledge or skills, or both. If skills are needed, you will need to incorporate practice into your workshop.
- Plan short sessions. People will retain skills more effectively if you modularize training in half-day lessons.
- Consider buying a packaged program if your development costs are high. Avoid packages that:
    - ✓ Cannot be customized
    - ✓ Have audiovisuals from a very different industry
    - ✓ Are aimed at a very different audience level
    - ✓ Are made in a foreign country
- Find out about your trainees. You should know:
    - ✓ Which previous courses they have taken

✓ What they need to know
✓ What they need to do better
✓ Their motivation level
✓ Their literacy level

- Develop materials to suit the audience. For example, materials for people with poor literacy should have more pictures and diagrams.
- Materials will be better if they:
  ✓ Contain one idea per page
  ✓ Are written in simple language
  ✓ Have lots of space to make notes
  ✓ Are interactive—have space for people to write answers, do quizzes, and complete checklists
- Book meeting rooms early. Advise attendees of location. Provide maps if necessary.

Before the Session

- Get to the training room early. Check your equipment.
- Arrange seating to suit the purpose of the session. Use:
  ✓ Theater style for a show-and-tell presentation
  ✓ U-shape for interactive training
  ✓ Round tables for teamwork exercises

At the Start of the Session

- Begin on a high note. Memorize the opening to start off strongly and set the tone for the workshop, or get a senior manager to start the workshop off.
- Mingle with participants to establish rapport.
- Develop a contract at the outset about what you expect of participants and what they can expect of you. Remind them that:
  ✓ They are responsible for their own learning
  ✓ They should let you know if their needs are not being met
  ✓ You will be starting and finishing on time
- Also, let people know about:
  ✓ Fire exits

✓ Telephone availability
✓ Washroom locations
✓ Break times
- Introduce yourself and get people to introduce themselves or have them interview one another. They can let everyone know their partner's:
  ✓ Name
  ✓ Job and special skills
  ✓ Key objectives
  ✓ Concerns about the workshop
- Make the objectives of the program clear. Post them where they can be seen clearly.
- Review the agenda so people are aware of how you are aiming to achieve your objectives.

During the Session

- Keep on schedule:
  ✓ Negotiate break lengths with participants.
  ✓ Note restarting times on the flipchart.
  ✓ Close the door at the agreed-upon starting time.
  ✓ Don't wait for stragglers.
  ✓ Don't summarize for people who come in late.
- If things don't go according to plan, don't raise awareness of the problem by apologizing.
- Don't be afraid to admit you don't have an answer to a question. Ask the others if they have the answer. If not, offer to get back to the person. Don't lie or wing it. Your integrity and honesty could be compromised, as well as your ability to influence the audience.
- Avoid using complex words such as *parameters*. Such words indicate that you are being theoretical and not down to earth.
- Use visuals wherever possible. They are six to eight times more effective than verbal instructions.
- Make sure that diagrams are culturally neutral.
- Stop from time to time to poll the audience. Ask, for example, "How many of you have tried this?" A poll provides a welcome change of pace and gives you useful information.

- Repeat or rephrase questions that are not heard by everyone in the audience.
- Vary the pace and presentation techniques as often as possible to keep interest at a high level. Remember, the attention span of most adults is about seven minutes. So change the tempo and presentation medium, and intersperse team tasks with individual assignments.
- Never show a video or conduct a lecture immediately after lunch since this is the time when people's energy drops to its lowest level. Instead, schedule:
  - ✓ A fun activity
  - ✓ Some physical exercises
- Draw information out of the group wherever possible. Their participation provides a change of pace and also validates your ideas in practical terms.
- End your workshop with a challenge. Ask everyone to commit to using some part of the workshop in the next two weeks. Conduct a survey, one person at a time, of what their intentions are.
- Ask people to write their action plans on a sheet of paper. Put these into self-addressed envelopes and mail them to participants sixty days after the workshop.

After the Session

- Evaluate your training not by how much people enjoyed your program but by whether they put the skills to use.
- Set up refresher courses, at which time you can confirm the effectiveness of the initial training, reinforce key skills, and add some new ones.

About the Author

Cy Charney, president of Charney and Associates Inc., is a leading consultant in the area of human resources management. He has developed significant change programs for many North American corporations in both the private and public sectors. His clients include Dun & Bradstreet, General Motors, Northern Telecom, TRW Aerospace, The Joint Commission for Health Care Accreditation, and the Workers' Compensation Board of British Columbia.

Cy is a frequent keynote speaker at conferences. He also customizes a variety of training programs for people at all levels in organizations. His most frequently delivered workshops include Facilitation Skills, Leadership, Negotiating Skills, Teamwork and Teambuilding, Running Effective Meetings, Problem Solving, Performance Management, Reengineering, Effective Supervision, and Total Quality Management.

As a consultant, Cy has helped many clients become leaders in their field. Through organizational reengineering, he has helped service, health, and manufacturing organizations meet the needs of their clients better, quicker, and at less cost.

Cy has published over a dozen articles as well as two books. *Quality Circles: A Guide to Participation and Productivity* deals with structured approaches to employee involvement; *Time to Market: Reducing Product Lead Time* focuses on techniques to make an organization more responsive.

Cy Charney is a psychology graduate and has a Master's Degree in Business Leadership. He also holds a P.Admin. designation from the Chartered Institute of Secretaries and Administrators, London. Born in South Africa and raised in Zimbabwe, Cy now lives in Toronto with his wife, Rhona, and children Daneal, Thalia, and Davin.